T0157260

Blessings of a Father
Education Contributions of Father Slattery
at Saint Finbarr's College

Blessings of a Father
Education Contributions of Father Slattery at Saint Finbarr's College

Deji Badiru

ABICS Publications
A Division of
AB International Consulting Services

www.ABICSPublications.com

Books for home, work, and leisure

Blessings of a Father

**Education Contributions of Father Slattery
at Saint Finbarr's College**

Deji Badiru

iUniverse, Inc.
Bloomington

Blessings of a Father
Education Contributions of Father Slattery at Saint Finbarr's College

Copyright © 2013 by Deji Badiru

All rights reserved. No part of this book may be used or reproduced by any means, graphic, electronic, or mechanical, including photocopying, recording, taping or by any information storage retrieval system without the written permission of the publisher except in the case of brief quotations embodied in critical articles and reviews.

iUniverse books may be ordered through booksellers or by contacting:

iUniverse
1663 Liberty Drive
Bloomington, IN 47403
www.iuniverse.com
1-800-Authors (1-800-288-4677)

Because of the dynamic nature of the Internet, any web addresses or links contained in this book may have changed since publication and may no longer be valid. The views expressed in this work are solely those of the author and do not necessarily reflect the views of the publisher, and the publisher hereby disclaims any responsibility for them.

Any people depicted in stock imagery provided by Thinkstock are models, and such images are being used for illustrative purposes only.

Certain stock imagery © Thinkstock.

ISBN: 978-1-4759-7049-4 (sc)
ISBN: 978-1-4759-7050-0 (e)

Printed in the United States of America

iUniverse rev. date: 1/7/2013

Dedication

This book is dedicated to the memory of my late sister, Mrs. Omowunmi Ayodele Durosimi (nee Badiru), to whom I refer as the "Minister of Education" for the Badiru family. She created the path that brought me into contact with Rev. Fr. Denis J. Slattery. May her soul rest in perfect peace.

"If I have seen further, it is by standing on the shoulders of giants."

- Sir Isaac Newton (1642 - 1727); English mathematician and philosopher

If I have accomplished anything, it is because I have been supported by the helpful hands of family, friends, and colleagues, and most importantly, by my wife, Iswat, who continues to stand by me through all my endeavors.

Professor and Mrs. Badiru in 2012

Contents

Preface

This book is about my time and positive educational experiences at Saint Finbarr's College, Akoka-Yaba, Lagos, Nigeria. With the passage of time, knowledge of the immense contributions of Father Slattery is moving into the deeper recesses of our memories. The purpose of this book is to revive and keep the memory alive for the benefit of future generations of students, teachers, parents, school administrators, and government officials in Nigeria.

This book, Blessings of a Father: Education Contributions of Father Slattery at Saint Finbarr's College, is a second and updated printing of the first edition, Blessings of a Father, first published in Nigeria in 2005. This current printing is intended to facilitate a wider and more archival distribution of the book, whose first edition received rave reviews. It is hoped that through this book and other dedicated archival manuscripts, the legacy of Father Denis J. Slattery and what the Catholic Church did for education in Nigeria shall never die.

Adedeji Badiru
January 1, 2013

Reverend Father Denis J. Slattery
February 29, 1916 – July 10, 2003

Preface from the First Edition

This book is not a biography of Rev. Fr. Denis J. Slattery, the founder and the first Principal of Saint Finbarr's College, Akoka, Lagos, Nigeria. It is not my own autobiography. Nor is it a representation of Saint Finbarr's College, the Catholic Mission in Nigeria, the Saint Finbarr's Old Boys Association, or the Saint Finbarr's Parents Teachers Association. The book represents my own personal memoirs, fond memories, and stories of the blessings that I received at Saint Finbarr's College through the work of Rev. Fr. Denis J. Slattery.

I believe the story is both interesting and motivational. I wanted to write the book for historical reasons as well as to serve as an inspiration to the present and future generations of Saint Finbarr's students. I hope this personal account will serve as a source of pride and encouragement to all those associated with Saint Finbarr's College --- the teachers, the students, the administrator, the parents, the Old Boys Association, and the Catholic Mission. The good work that Father Slattery started in 1956 must continue through the efforts of others. I hope my story can serve as one of the bonds that will continue to unite the various groups who have dedicated themselves to the continuation and betterment of Saint Finbarr's College. I need to write this story so that those who know me may understand why I am passionate about educational opportunities and pursuits as well as my commitment to opening doors for others.

I thank the Almighty God for giving me the means through which I could successfully carry out the challenge of writing this book. The fact that I am able to do this is a manifestation of the blessings of Father Slattery. There are many other stories similar to mine, and I hope this book will encourage others to write and disseminate their own stories. It is the only way we can ensure a lasting legacy of Rev. Fr. Denis Slattery.

One major lesson that I learned from Father Slattery was the fact that the material things of the world are immaterial when it comes to how the world will remember you. He taught us that what matters is how we touch the lives of others. This explains how I have conducted my professional life over the past several decades. I have tried to dedicate myself to finding even the smallest of ways to touch the lives of others. It is my belief and hope that those that I have had an opportunity to help will deem it right to help others. Such transmittable goodwill is what the world needs to continue to be beneficial to everyone. Following the lessons of Father Slattery, I dedicated myself to writing *Blessings of a Father* so that others can appreciate the benefits of infectious goodwill. This book will help to preserve Father Slattery's deeds for posterity.

All the proceeds from the sale of this book will go directly to Saint Finbarr's College in support of future PTA projects at the school.

First Edition: Badiru, Adedeji B., Blessings of a Father: A tribute to the Life and Work of Reverend Father Denis J. Slattery, Henriz Designs & Prints, Lagos, Nigeria, 2005.

Acknowledgments

I thank all those who have, in the past and in the present, continued to support my dedication to preserving and publicizing the legacy of Saint Finbarr's College, Akoka, Yaba, Lagos, Nigeria. I particularly thank my co-members of Saint Finbarr's College Old Boys Association – North America. Of particular mention and re-mention is the duo of Kenny Kuku and John Nwofia. Boys, the dedication continues!

Acknowledgments to the First Edition

I wish to express my profound gratitude to friends, family, and colleagues who have given me all manners of support over the years. I have harboured the wish to write this book for several years. All these supporters have heard my countless verbal expressions of wanting to tell my Saint Finbarr's story. Only now have I had the opportunity to turn the wish into a reality.

There are too many people to name in the acknowledgments for this book. But I would be remiss not to mention some specific names. I immensely thank my wife, **Iswat**, for putting up with my obsession with Saint Finbarr's. After 30 years of being married to me, she still wonders how I never get tired of talking about my experiences at Saint Finbarr's College. I was so consumed by the urge to write this book that my wife thought it portended a peril to my other responsibilities. She is glad that now that the book has been written, we may finally have some quiet in the household. She expects me to let people read the book, rather than my telling the story verbally endlessly. But the story of Father Slattery and Saint Finbarr's College has to continue to be told. So, I cannot pledge silence from now on.

I thank all my friends for continuing to listen, appreciate, and respect my Saint Finbarr's story. As I recall some special background events leading to the writing of this book, I must express thanks to **Mr. F. B. Odunayo, Mr. Supo "Busco" Adedeji**, and **Prof. Oye Ibidapo-Obe**. I thank **Mr. Segun Ajanlekoko**, whose unparalleled leadership of the Saint Finbarr's College Old Boys Association for many years provided a major inspiration to me to press on with the book project. I thank my former Saint Finbarr's classmate, **Mr. Philip Bieni**, whose brotherly love has facilitated linkages and reunion of Saint Finbarr's Old Boys in the USA. Over all these years, he has continued a "search and retrieve" effort to locate our Old Boys in the USA. I thank my children, Abidemi, Adetokunboh, and Omotunji for lending their listening ears. While growing up in the household, Abi and Ade always found it amusing whenever I insisted on passing on my Saint Finbarr's lessons to them. Even though times have changed and lessons can no longer be imparted in the old-fashioned way, I am convinced some of my old lessons have rubbed on them positively. My rule to them is simple: "Respect yourself so that other people can respect you."

I thank all my former teachers at Saint Finbarr's College, who gave me fond memories of my times at the school. Particularly close were my French, Art, and Biology teachers from 1968 through 1972. I thank my former professors in the USA, **Prof. Sid Gilbreath, Prof. Gary Whitehouse**, and **Prof. Carroll Viera**, whose teachings and supportive caring contributed greatly to the shaping of my post-Finbarr's life.

Writing a book of this magnitude is an enormous undertaking. It requires extraordinary coordination, beyond what I can handle by myself from abroad. I thank **Mrs. Anu Koleowo** for serving as the coordinator for this book project. I thank **Mr. Joe Igbokwe** for his creative writing and contribution of a chapter to help bridge my Finbarr's story with the bigger issue of what obtains in our educational and social systems.

I thank my administrative support staff, **Jeanette Myers,** proofreader, **Em Turner Chitty,** and typesetting consultant, **Mary Ann Venable,** for fine-tuning and typesetting the draft of the manuscript of this book.

I thank all those others who participated directly or indirectly in the actualization of this book. Space limitation prevents me from listing all the names deserving to be listed. Please take comfort in the fact that I recognize all of you.

Above all, I acknowledge the memory of my late mother, **Madam Rukayat Badiru.** While I was on my educational sojourn abroad, she endured the pains of waiting, consoled only by the joy of hope. The hope eventually materialized via the incipient blessings of Father Slattery.

Appreciation goes to the list of Testimony Contributors:

Segun Ajanlekoko
Philip Bieni
Joe Igbokwe
John Nwofia
Donatus Oguamanam
F. B. A. Ogundipe
R. T. N. Onyeje

The Catalyst for Writing the First Edition

I had toyed with the idea of writing this book for several years. But the demands of other priorities and commitments made it impossible until a chance encounter with a final catalyst on December 14, 2004. I had just attended the convocation event at the University of Lagos and was driving by Saint Finbarr's College on my way back to the Gbagada area. This is a frequent route that I had taken many times when visiting Lagos. On previous drive-bys, I always glanced, with a depressed heart, at the dilapidated condition of the buildings on the college campus. The transfer of the school to the Lagos State Government in the mid-1970s has led to disheartening decline of the physical infrastructure of the school. I and several Old Boys of the school often lamented the miserable condition of the school and we had sought ways to contribute to the revitalization and upkeep of the school. But such efforts had been scanty and disjointed for many years, primarily because the government authorities were not interested in or supportive of the isolated efforts of Old Boys Associations throughout the state. But the return of the mission schools to the religious missions in October 2001 opened the way for several self-help opportunities for the mission schools. Consequently, the Catholic Mission and the PTA (Parent-Teacher Association) had embarked on several revitalization projects at Saint Finbarr's College. So, on this fateful date of December 14, 2004, I noticed a marked difference in the external appearance of the school.

Intrigued, I asked my driver to stop so that I could snap a few pictures of the external structures of the school. Upon exiting the car, I noticed more of the freshly painted main gates and building walls of the school. The broken glass panes that had previously been notoriously visible from the jumbled lanes of Akoka Road had been replaced. Encouraged by the appealing and inviting appearance, I stepped through the open main gates onto the compounds of the school. An immediate rush of nostalgia overcame me. I was metaphorically transformed into the old period of my attendance at the school. It was late afternoon and school had already ended for the day. There were no pupils around. But security guards and teachers were around the compound. The initial plan to snap only a few pictures became an engagement of snapping several pictures. I think the security guards were taken aback. They just watched me as I snapped one picture of the compound after another. I had a digital camera with me. So, there was no concern of running out of film. Undaunted, I stepped deeper into the school premises. The security guards continued to watch me more closely. But they never raised any objection. I believe they figured that I must be some special person, considering the boldness with which I stepped onto the compound. After a cursory, but courteous, salutation to the guards, I just started snapping pictures. They probably thought that I was an agent of some higher authority and did not want to risk a confrontation. So, I continued my merry photographing of the school. I zoomed in on the freshly painted caption, ART ROOM, above the door to the room, which I still recognized as the art room where I spent countless hours preparing for my School Certificate Art examination. Art was one of my selected subjects for school certificate in 1972. The Art Room held special memories for me, as readers will find out in a later chapter of this book.

Anyway, the taking of pictures continued unabashed. However, upon reaching the inner courtyard containing the block where my former Class 5A was located, I was finally confronted by a lady who introduced herself as **Mrs. Perpetual Aligwara**, a history teacher at the school. She wanted to know who I was because she noticed the special interest I was directing at the buildings as I took the pictures. I introduced myself as a Saint Finbarr's College Old Boy from the early 1970s. She was intrigued by my obvious sentimental attachment to the school premises. She invited me into the teachers' office complex and wanted to introduce me to the new school administrator, **Rev. Fr. J. G. Oduntan**. But Father Oduntan was not available at that time. Mrs. Aligwara insisted that I must find time to come back to meet Father Oduntan. I informed her that I was visiting Lagos only briefly and would be traveling back to the USA by that weekend. She then told me that if I could come back on Thursday, December 16, 2004, I could meet Father Oduntan and other important people associated with the school. That day was the scheduled date for the official commissioning of PTA projects at the school. I was ecstatic about the opportunity to participate in such an important event. I felt lucky to have walked into the opportunity to witness, first-hand, the new happenings at the school. I thanked Mrs. Aligwara for the information and promised her that I would come back on Thursday. I did not bother to take any more pictures at that point.

Because I knew I would be back to partake in more photo opportunities, I rearranged my schedules for the remaining days in Lagos and I was able to attend the commissioning events. My plan was to position myself on the fringes of the events and just snap pictures. But once Mrs. Aligwara spotted me in the audience, she immediately informed Father Oduntan, who motioned to everyone to bring me under the tent to join the special guests. Father Oduntan received me very warmly. As I sat under the tent, the joy that flowed through my veins was unbelievable, as I watched the present crop of Saint Finbarr's College students. I felt like jumping into their midst to relive the good old days that I had at Saint Finbarr's College. I watched and took in every movement of the students, the teachers, and the administrators. Members of my own entourage, consisting of my brother, Mr. Biodun Badiru, my administrative staff, Joke Odutayo, and support staff, Mr. Wale Adesanya, were ushered under another tent so that they could be appropriately catered to. It was a beautiful commissioning programme. It was very well organized and choreographed, with plenty of food and drinks for everyone. I was filled with a sense of commendation for the PTA for putting on such a remarkable programme of events. I appreciated all the efforts of all the various people engaged in creating a proud moment for Saint Finbarr's College.

It was at that point that I reiterated to myself the commitment to write this book. I knew that if I didn't write the book at this opportune time, I might never have another chance to write it. Fortunately, the holiday period of 2004 was just around the corner. I took the opportunity of using that period to start writing the book.

I thought of ways that I could contribute to the revitalization efforts of the school. My pledge of support is to direct all the proceeds of this book to go directly to the school in support of future PTA projects. The PTA has done a fantastic job through their own initiative and it deserves and needs the support of those who are able to render support. It is my hope that we can make Saint Finbarr's College a perpetual testament of the wide-ranging contributions of Father Slattery to education in Nigeria.

Ode to Reverend Father Denis Joseph Slattery

Our father is gone;
Our father is gone;
Our Reverend Father Slattery is gone;
Even though he is no longer with us;
His blessings continue to guide us.
Nature propagates life; mankind finds ways to diminish it.
Throughout his life, Father Slattery pursued ways to rectify the
errors of mankind.

Father Slattery wearing ceremonial chieftaincy attire in
Nigeria (Circa 1960)

School Anthem of Saint Finbarr's College

Saint Finbarr's College
My own alma mater
I am proud to belong
I am proud to belong
To the citadel of excellence

Fidelitas (2ce)
Fidelitas

School Pledge

I pledge to
Saint Finbarr's College as a worthy student
To be loyal to the college Authorities
To respect and cooperate with all staff and Prefects of the college
And obey all rules and regulations of the college
To project the college with pride in good light everywhere and at all times, and
To do all in my power to leave the College better than I met it,
So, help me God.

Assembly Hall Song

(Note: This was a popular assembly-hall song at Saint Finbarr's in the 1970s)

Hail Queen Of Heaven (sing):

Hail, Queen of heaven, the ocean star,
Guide of the wanderer here below,
Thrown on life's surge, we claim thy care,
Save us from peril and from woe.

Mother of Christ, O Star of the sea
Pray for the wanderer, pray for me.

Main Entrance to Saint Finbarr's College,
Akoka-Yaba, Lagos, Nigeria

Recitation Performance by Finbarr's Pupils,
December 16, 2004

Saint Finbarr's College Heritage

Saint Finbarr's College has spread its tentacles around the world. Several "old boys" of the school are now in key productive and influential positions around the world. Like other storied high schools in Nigeria, Finbarr's has made significant contributions in human resource development in Nigeria. But one distinct and unmistakable fact about Finbarr's is that it has a unifying force -- Rev. Fr. Denis Slattery; the man and the name. Every time we hear the name, a refreshing chill still runs down our spines.

All graduates of Saint Finbarr's College remain very proud of the school's heritage. Father Slattery encouraged each person to embrace whatever his family religion dictated; but he demanded the study of the Bible as a source of well-rounded education. Thus, Bible Religious Studies was a core subject at the school. Father taught his students to enjoy the thrills and perils of playing sports as a preparation for the other challenges of life. The discipline received from the school has served us very well. It is probably the single most important factor in the professional and personal success of our "Old Boys."

In the Yoruba language, Finbarrians are fondly referred to as "Omo Slattery," meaning Slattery's children. Yes, he was our father both in the figurative sense as well as in the spiritual sense.

Father Slattery trained us to be what we are and his lesson still lives on in everyone of us. Although his service was primarily in Nigeria, his good example should be publicized to serve other parts of the world. To the last man, every Finbarrian (former and present) has the unity of purpose to disseminate the glory of Saint Finbarr's College, Akoka, Lagos, Nigeria.

Deji Badiru's Advice to the Ambitious:

"Don't use people as rungs for your ladder of success."

A Cherished Blessing

A December 1998 Christmas Card from Father Slattery to the Badiru Family contains his usual statements of blessings. The card remains a cherished item in the family's collection of memorable items. The greetings, in Father Slattery's own aged handwriting, reads as follows:

"Dear Adedeji B. Badiru

Congratulations for all the letters from U.S. and also thank you for the video. Received it here in Ireland on Twenty-third November 1998.

I hope a member of my family will tape it and send a copy to our Boss – Blackrock Road, Cork. It will be kept in the Archives and probably used occasionally to help the cause of the Mission.

I was very proud of all the old boys who appeared on the video. Your speeches were wonderful. You made it a historic and unique occasion.

You will be happy to know that I am all set for my return journey to Lagos –

I hope to continue for some time the work of the Mission and pay a special attention to Finbarr's and the old boys and the new.

Thanks for all you have done for the Alma Mater.

Greet your wife and children. May God Bless you all.

Happy and holy Christmas.

God bless you.

Denis Slattery"

Chapter One
In The Beginning

In order to understand how Saint Finbarr's College transformed my life, one needs to know my own beginning and early years and how I came to cross paths with Rev. Fr. Slattery. I overcame several educational adversities before reaching my present educational attainment. Glory be to the good God.

The Journey Began

I was born on September 2nd, 1952, into the Sharafa Ola Badiru Onisarotu family of Epe, Lagos State. By the standard of the day, it was an affluent family. My father was a building contractor and traveled extensively in pursuit of his profession. Several of his children were, thus, born outside of Epe. He was a particularly popular person at Okegbogi Street in Ondo township in the late 1940s and early 1950s. I was only five years old when my father died prematurely on April 12, 1958. Thus, began the family hiatus that would disrupt what would have otherwise been a steady and sheltered upbringing. Because of his sudden death, his family was not prepared for how to manage and care for the younger children in the large family.

Fortunately, we had some grown children among us at that time. The adult children in the family "distributed" the younger ones among themselves to see to their upbringing. In the process, I was shuttled from one place to another, from one sibling to another, and from one extended relative to another. Over a period of a few years, I stayed with brothers, sisters, uncles, and some distant relatives. I had the good fortune of having a large and extended family with no shortage of good Samaritans willing to take me on as a ward.

A Late Starter

The result of being a migrant ward was that I could not start school until 1961 --- at the late age of nine! I started elementary school as Zumratul Islamiyyah Elementary school at No. 2, Tawaliu Bello Street, adjacent to Nnamdi Azikwe Road in the heart of Lagos in 1961. Thus, my first encounter with counting 1, 2, 3 and reciting A, B, C was not until I was nine years old. This late start, coupled with the fact that I started school in Lagos, where primary education was for eight years (in those days) compared to six years in the Western region, meant that I was five years behind my educational cohorts. But one thing that was in my favor at that time was my maturity level. At that age, I already understood the importance of education. I did not need any prodding or forcing to go to school. My level of maturity made me more attentive and appreciative of the teachers in the classroom. So, I was able to take in all lessons presented by the teachers. I did not need any supplementary lessons outside of school. In those days, teachers and observers erroneously attributed my better school performance (compared to my classmates) to my higher level of intelligence. For a long time, I mistakenly believed it too. But what was actually fueling the better academic performance was my higher maturity level. I enjoyed excellent rapport with my classmates and teachers. I could tell that the teachers not only liked me, but also respected me. For this reason, I never got into any punishment episode at school. I went through the entire elementary school without ever being flogged at school, in an age when school flogging was very rampant. The same record was later repeated throughout my secondary school years.

Relations to the Rescue

I suffered enough flogging at the homes of my guardians (for being rascally) to make up for the grace that I enjoyed at school. Contrary to the typical situation in those days, the school was my refuge. I enjoyed going to school in order to escape what I considered to be very oppressive home environment. It happened that what, as a child, I considered to be oppressive chores at home turned out to be valuable lessons that still continue to serve me well at home until today. I still remain very handy at home, particularly in the kitchen. My adoption of school as a refuge was fortuitous because it paved the way for my sound academic foundation. I knew I would not be able to study at home so I paid every bit of attention to the lectures at school. That way, I imbibed everything the teacher had to say. I never had an opportunity for supplementary lessons or studying at home. I relied entirely on school lectures. I could not afford not to pay attention at school. Children nowadays have the luxury of private lessons. Sometimes they get too lackadaisical about the opportunities.

In those days, I tended to have a free-wheeling lifestyle of freedom to roam the neighbourhood streets in search of play and fun. This did not sit well with my guardians, who preferred for me to be indoors to attend to household chores. So, I was frequently on a collision course with my guardians about my over-commitment to playing around the neighborhood. In spite of this rascally disposition, I still enjoyed good relationships with my guardians primarily because I still performed well in school. I recall an elderly neighbour intervening and pleading with one of my guardians to spare me a flogging on account of my school performance. He opined that, in spite of my playing too much, I was still doing very well at school compared to my playmates, who were playing and not doing well at school.

One of my favorite guardians was my uncle, the late Chief Alao Shabi. I learnt a lot of calm demeanor and rational mode of speaking from him. Although he flogged me a few times also, it was always at the instigation of unfair reports getting to him about what and what offense I had committed. Typical reports were about my being seen riding a bicycle around the neighbourhood, swimming in a local public pool, or playing football on the playground. These were all considered dangerous and unauthorized acts in those days. That some of us learnt to ride bicycles, swim, and play football was a credit to our mischievous acts of running away from home for a few hours to engage in these fun but "dangerous" acts. My uncle was a scrap-metal dealer. He had a scrap-metal shop at Idumagbo in the heart of Lagos in the 1960s. His shop was later moved to Owode Onirin in the outskirts of Lagos. From 1965 through 1967, I helped him to tend the scrap metal shop along with his Hausa assistant, named Gaji. The general expectation was that after elementary school, I would become a full-time apprentice to my uncle and eventually go into the scrap metal business, which was a lucrative business in those days. My uncle engaged in exporting scrap metals overseas. So, he interacted with white expatriates through the ports at Apapa. The decades following Nigeria's independence saw a decline in the lucrative level of scrap metals. If I had gone into that business, I would probably be mired in the economic depression associated with it now.

I learnt a lot of hands-on activities from Gaji. He was the one who first introduced me to the properties of various metals and how to handle them. He gave me an early (albeit unscientific) appreciation for various metals. We sorted scrap metals into their respective categories. We dealt with mercury, silver, iron, steel, copper, brass, platinum, and other metals. I don't recall handling gold in those days. The hands-on skills still serve me well today in handling household tools. Even now, my most cherished possessions are the implements of household work such as hammers, pliers, screw drivers, drills, and so on. Anyone visiting my home now can hardly miss my intimate relationships with these implements.

The Search for a Secondary School

I graduated from elementary school in 1967 and was to enter secondary school in January 1968. Because of my good academic performance and excellent result in the common entrance examination, it was generally believed that I would not encounter any difficulty in gaining admission into a secondary school. But there were other obstacles lurking beneath the raw academic record. What I thought should not matter in gaining admission into a reputable school (befitting of my common entrance results) were actually major obstacles in the eyes of the secondary school officials.

The prospects of not being able to pay school fees preempted my being admitted to the most reputable secondary schools. My sister, the late Mrs. Omowunmi Ayodele Durosimi (previously Mrs. Shojobi), insisted that I must go to a reputable high school because of her belief and confidence in my academic promise. She had monitored my performance throughout my elementary school and concluded that nothing but the best schools were appropriate for me. She, herself, had attended Queens School, Ede, in the Western Region. She had the vision of my attending such schools such as Kings College, Government College, and other well-known schools. Well, I applied to all those schools. Based on my common entrance examination results, I was invited for interview at all the schools. I was self-assured and confident about my academic-related performance at the interviews. But I was naïve about the other factors that were considered in admitting children to those schools. Frequently,

5

at those interviews, I had no shoes on and wore the simplest of clothes. Being more mature than the other kids seeking admission, I always attended the interviews by myself. No accompanying parents, siblings, or relatives. If I had asked my family members, I could have received appropriate support to put on an "air" of being well-off enough to attend the schools. But I made a deliberate and conscious decision to attend the interview just as I was – without any pretensions. I was somehow arrogant about my academic capabilities, and I believed the school authorities would be impressed. But I was very wrong. My attitude going into the interviews was that I wanted to challenge the interviewers to ask me any question about school subjects so that I could impress them with my knowledge. But very often, questions were raised only about tangential elements that had nothing to do with school subjects. Some typical questions that I faced (and failed) were:

Who will pay your school fees?
Where is your father's house?
Did your mother attend a secondary school?
Has anybody in your family attended this school before?
Is your mother a trader or a government worker?
What is your professional goal?
Which elementary school did you attend?
Have you ever attended a nursery school?

The interviewers thought I would be a misfit at an Ivy-League type of secondary school. Although Zumratul Islamiyyah Elementary School was a good school on the inside, it was not highly regarded externally. This could be because it was located in the rough and tough inner-city part of Lagos Island. The street address of No. 2 Tawaliu Bello Street, adjacent to Nnamidi Azikwe Road, was noted more for commercial activities rather than as an academic base for a well-regarded school.

I had no doubt the other kids had been well-coached about the interview questions and had well-honed answers for all such silly questions. But I was brash and determined not to stoop too low as to give answers that would amount to pretensions. My sister had expected that many schools would be so impressed with my academic performance that they would admit me with scholarship offers. So, there was no prior arrangement or preparation by my family regarding how to pay my school fees. Frankly, my sister was caught off guard by the disappointing admission outcomes.

To be somewhat fair to the interviewers, my older age probably played against me. There I was trying to enter a secondary school at the ripe age of 16. I was five years older than my contemporaries seeking admission at the same time. Not knowing my history of starting school very late (at the age of 9), the interviewers very likely equated my advanced age to being slow in the elementary school. Their natural suspicion of my being academically dim did not match the documented performance on paper. So, they probably decided to err on the side of caution.

Zumratul did not have a secondary school at that time. Otherwise, I would have been a shoo-in to progress from Zumratul Elementary School to Zumratul Secondary School. So, I was like a goldfish out of a backyard pond looking to be placed in an ivy-league aquarium.

That I even attended Zumratul Elementary School had been by accident rather than by design. At my age of nine years in 1961, elementary schools were reluctant to enroll me. I was a raw and untested pupil with no prior preparation to enter school. The "raw" part of me at that time was what led to my moniker of "BB Raw-Raw" later on. BB stands for my middle and last names -- Bodunde Badiru. I proudly autographed that insignia on my early drawings and paintings. The full salutation was

"BB Raw-Raw, Broken Bottle Never Tires." Whatever that was supposed to mean, I never knew. Many of my early friends still call me BB; but most people have forgotten or never knew of the Raw-Raw part of the motto.

In the search for my first elementary school, it happened that a sister-in-law, the late Mrs. Shadiyat Badiru, wife of my late brother, Mr. Atanda Badiru, was a book seller at the school at the time that an elementary school was being sought for me. She took me to the principal, who queried me about why I was just entering school for the first time. I was able to give him satisfactory answers because I was old enough to be cognizant of my situation and the consequences of my predicament. The principal was very impressed with my mature communication abilities. He decided to enroll me, jokingly making a comment that "Enu e dun," which satirically meant that my stories were enticing.

In 1967, I was invited to several Secondary School admission interviews. Notable among these were King's College, Lagos and Government College, Ibadan. None of these were successful. Even though the interview experiences were not successful, they were, nonetheless, very gratifying. The honor of being invited to interview at those schools brought much pride and joy to the officials of my elementary school. The interview at Government College, Ibadan, was a protracted one-week affair that culminated in written and oral tests on various subjects. I was informed that I did very well on the tests but did not meet the cut-off requirements in the overall interview. I returned to Lagos empty-handed.

A Search for Help

After attending several interviews and not being successful, I concluded that I needed a better answer to the question of "Who will pay your school fees?" So, I embarked on an effort of seeking financial support from local philanthropists. One noted person that I appealed to was the late Chief S. B. Bakare. I had heard of several philanthropic projects that he had undertaken. I was hopeful that he would be so impressed by my academic potential that he might want to invest in my education. So, I crafted a well-written letter to him explaining my plight. The letter included carefully composed paragraphs that would indicate to him my knowledge and command of the English language, even at that age. I included statements about my common entrance exam results. I never received a response.

My disappointment was contained only by the prospects of contacting other philanthropists in Lagos. There was no shortage of such benefactors in Lagos in those days. Unfortunately, none of them came my way. All my attempts at pursuing philanthropic grace were futile. Years later, I began to understand why I might not have heard from those that I contacted. It could have been that they never received my letters at all because I did not have the correct addresses. It could also have been that their administrative assistants obstructed the delivery of the letters. Perhaps, they received thousands of requests, beyond what they could comfortably respond to or provide financial assistance for.

Chapter Two
Admission to Saint Finbarr's College

My admission to Saint Finbarr's College was nothing short of a miracle. After several months on searching for a secondary school without success, the family's attention turned to exploring other options for my future. There were discussions of my going into some trade apprenticeship. A popular option was for me to capitalize on my drawing skills by going into a sign-writing business. Imagine the caption, "BB Raw-Raw Signs" or "BB, the Sign Writer" on a roadside kiosk.

Rescued by a Sister

That Saint Finbarr's College was considered as an option was due to a fortunate act of geographical proximity. I was living with my sister at the University of Lagos Staff Quarters at that time. She was then married to Dr. Wole Shojobi, who was then a Civil Engineering lecturer at the University. Having found no school yet, my sister decided that we should consider one of the local schools on the mainland of Lagos. Thus, Saint Finbarr's College came into the picture. Being in the immediate vicinity of Unilag, Finbarr's was a convenient choice.

The school was appealing because it was close and did not have a boarding school. Attending a boarding school far away would have compounded my financial inability to pay the school fees. My sister contacted Saint Finbarr's College and found out that there might be some openings in the school. It was already two weeks after school session started in January 1968. The fact that any openings existed at that time was a fortuitous coincidence. The school was looking for a few additional good students and I was looking for one good school. My sister sent me to the school to inquire. As usual, I went to the school all by myself.

First Encounter of a Fatherly Kind

It was a good thing that Reverend Father Slattery did not care what a prospective student looked like. I went to the school without shoes and no impressive "garmentry." Unlike my previous secondary school interview experiences, Father Slattery attended to me the same way he attended to all the parents who had come to the school with their kids to inquire about the "rumoured" openings. The Father was quite an impressive and blessed being. Although it was the first time that I would speak directly to a white man, I completely understood him and he understood me perfectly. I believe this is a credit to his years of living in Nigeria and communicating with various categories of Nigerians in local communities. He announced to everyone that there were **only three** vacancies. He cautioned that no parent should approach him to lobby for the open positions. He was going to fill the three vacancies purely on the basis of merit. There were several parents and kids in the audience when the announcement was made. I was the only unaccompanied boy in the group. By my own estimate, there must have been at least two hundred boys. I concluded that I had no chance, and presumed this to be another disappointing outcome in my lengthy and lonely search for a secondary school.

How was Father Slattery going to ensure a fair process of selecting only three kids from the hundreds that were interested in being admitted? He laughed at the parents' inquiry. He responded that he had an ingenious plan. He told everyone to come back on some specified date. He did not say what the selection plan was. I believe he kept the plan secret to preempt any attempt by any parent to usurp the process. Without knowing the selection process, no one knew how to prepare or scheme for success. He told everyone there was no need for the kids to prepare anything for the appointed date. Just show up on time. Disappointed, everyone left for that day. I was filled with misgivings about the whole thing. But I was heartened by the fact that I was still in the running.

Father's Grand Admission Plan

On the appointed day, I showed up at the school, unaccompanied, as usual. Father Slattery told everyone to assemble in the open field across from the Assembly Hall. There were hundreds of anxious eyes. There were murmerings among the parents regarding what was going on; and what was going to happen. Father Slattery stepped onto the high concrete pavement bordering the Assembly Hall. This position gave him an elevated view of the audience. It was like being on a high-rise podium. After positioning himself majestically in front of and above the audience, he announced that he was going to select three kids from the audience to fill the open vacancies on the basis of the common entrance exam results. Everyone was baffled. How was he going to do that? Father asked two clerks from the school office to come onto the pavement. A table and a chair were hurriedly positioned on the pavement. The clerks had been inside the Assembly Hall (as if on a secret mission), waiting for Father's instruction to emerge. After the clerks were appropriately settled, with one sitting on the chair and the other standing beside the table with papers and pencils in hand, Father Slattery beckoned to the school secretary, I believe her name was Monica, to bring out a big pile of typed sheets, the like of which I had never seen until then. The pile must have measured almost one foot above the table. People in the audience looked at one another anxiously. No one knew what was about to unfold.

As I would become aware later on during my days at Saint Finbarr's, Father Slattery's antics at getting things done often bordered on craziness. He was a renegade of a person. He had a penchant for the unexpected. His ways of doing things were replete with surprises, wonderment, curiosity, and suspense. He could have been a successful movie star.

He would always find unusual and amusing ways to get things done. I think that was by a deliberate design by him. Through his unconventional approach, he got a lot of attention. Once he got your attention, he could then impose his will on you. People were often amused, rather than being offended, by his unusual and eccentric ways. He had a volatile temperament to match his odd ways. But no one dared challenge him. So, everyone waited patiently for him to announce his grand plan. He hesitated in announcing his plan deliberately to keep the audience in suspense and partly to disarm any rancor from the audience. Father Slattery often operated like a shrewd psychologist. He had all kinds of ingenious means of dealing with people. That was why he was so beloved throughout Nigeria. I don't think he ever lost an argument in his heydays. When discussions didn't go his way, he would put on a fake tantrum in order to still get his way. People usually succumbed to him by simply laughing in amazement of his antics. He was an all-encompassing person: a Revered Clergyman, a comic (if need be), a humorist (if necessary to lighten the moment), a runner (chasing after mischievous kids), a boxer (if needed to mete out a punishment), and a sportsman to the core. Except for his clergy robes, his restless ways revealed no sign that he was a Catholic priest. It

13

was not until his later years, in a slowed state of physical being, that anyone could rein him in.

Well, with all the suspense over, Father Slattery announced that the clerks would start reading names off the pile of common entrance examination results. The pile of computer paper contained the list of common entrance results in merit order. Names would be read from the list until the three highest scoring boys in the audience were identified. This process was baffling because there was no way to ensure when the three names would be found among those kids in the audience. Father maintained that if all the kids in the audience had taken the common entrance examination in Lagos State, then their names would appear somewhere in the list of results, even if they were at the far end of the list. Father Slattery said he was prepared to continue this exercise until the highest three had been identified, even if it took days. Being enmeshed in the crowd, I could hear hisses from some parents. Were they prepared to commit that kind of indefinite time, with no assurance of success in the end? Some parents tried to get Father's attention for private discussions. But he refused. Even the highly-placed, obviously rich, and well-connected parents in the audience could not sway Father Slattery from his determined approach. Many parents tensely tried to explain the process to their kids. Being alone, I had no one to explain anything to me. Instead, I eavesdropped on the covert mumblings deep within the recesses of the crowd.

Unconcerned, Father Slattery motioned to the clerks to start reading out the names. So it was that we embarked on this journey of the seemingly endless reading of names. I started praying fervently inwardly to be one of the three selected. Being of small stature, and having only myself to account for, I gradually pushed my way to the front of the crowd. I positioned myself right in front of the clerks' table. I was occasionally pushed back by one of the clerks, wanting to create sufficient elbow room for the prevailing task. At one time, Father Slattery threatened to end the process if the audience crowded the clerks too closely. But realizing the anxiety among the audience, he relented. So, my position was secured very close to the face of the person reading the names.

The Chosen Few

Names were read on and on. The process went on for several hours without anyone acknowledging the names read so far. Being at the edge of the table, I could scan each page of the list as soon as the clerk opened it, before the reading of that page started. When my name was not on the list, I would pray silently so that no one else in the audience would be on that page. The process had started around 9a.m. It must have been around 1p.m. when the first name from the audience was found. The first successful name found was Francis Egbuniwe.

So, one position out of three was gone. I had only two more chances of entering Saint Finbarr's College. I intensified my silent prayers. But instead of being picked second, someone else was picked to fill the next open position. The second successful name found was Joseph Molokwu.

After what seemed like more endless hours, I spotted my name about the middle of a newly opened page. I screamed, "That's my name, that's my name, on this page, that's my name." "My name is here!," sticking my finger at my name listed on the page. This unauthorized announcement caught everyone off guard. I was shouted at to keep quiet. Names must be read from the top to the bottom. There would be no interjection to the middle of the page. When the clerk got to that point, the name would be called. So, I kept quiet as chided. I further intensified my silent prayers. "God, let no one else be called ahead of my name on that page." I am sure that the Good Lord was listening to my juvenile prayers. The third, and final successful name found was Bodunde Badiru.

Although the passage of time has eroded my recollection of the exact events of that day, the agony of the tense waiting has remained etched in my memory. In later years at the school, Francis, Joseph, and I, along with Joseph's close friend, Michael Elumeze, would engage in endless debates as to who was picked first, second, or third. I still feel the torment of waiting to be picked third. So, I remember the order clearly. Father Slattery came back onto the scene to formalize the selection of the three kids. He announced that these three kids,

Francis Egbuniwe,
Joseph Molokwu, and
Bodunde Badiru,

were the new students of Saint Finbarr's College. They must show up to start classes in the morning, without delay. School had already started two weeks earlier. So, we must start attending classes forthwith.

Thus, I began my secondary school education at Saint Finbarr's College in January 1968. Father Slattery handled the admission process his own way. It was fair, just, and transparent. It was right there in the open field. No flattery, no pretensions. There were no private meetings. There were no under-the-table deals. It was the only way I could have entered a reputable secondary school in 1968. All other doors had been slammed shut. Father Slattery opened the door of educational opportunity for me, without consideration of age, colour, creed, race, tribe, language, financial status, political leaning, or religious affiliation. It was totally on the basis of merit. He let the best in the pool of prospective students rise to the top to claim the three prized positions. Can you see my point now? It was a special blessing for me. I hope readers can now understand why writing this book is very special to me. I cannot imagine going to my grave without committing this story to a published book. I am extraordinarily indebted to Father Slattery. Writing this book is the only way I can reward his kindness and fairness. Leaders of today and tomorrow should learn a lot from Father Slattery's ways.

Chapter Three
Denis Slattery, the Man and
the Reverend Father

To further appreciate my story, the reader must understand the background of Rev. Fr. Denis Slattery, the Irish priest who touched the lives of many Nigerians. He was an exceptional human being from the time he was born on 29th February, 1916 until his death on 10th July, 2003.

"Slattery, no flattery!" The writer Ochereome Nnanna presented this accurate characterization of Father Slattery in a 1996 newspaper editorial on People & Politics in celebration of Father Slattery's 80th birthday. All the accolades that Father Slattery has received over the years, both while he was alive and following his death, contain the same unmistakable fact. There was never any flattery about him. He was a man of no pretensions. What you saw was what you got from him. I have tried to pattern myself after him in that regard. A friend once called me "Deji of no pretensions." I still cherish that characterization.

Father Slattery prided himself as an Irish-Nigerian and has been credited with many contributions to the development of modern

Nigeria (both pre-independence and following independence). He was a patriot to the core, an activist for righteousness not only from the standpoint of religion, but also from the points of social equality and political self-determination. His 1996 Memoirs, *My Life Story*, published by West African Book Publishers, Ltd. gives a very detailed account of his contributions to Nigeria and Nigerians.

One admirable attribute of his work in Nigeria was his commitment to a non-parochial view of issues. He supported the views of different religious leanings, as long as the views matched the tenets of good citizenship. There was religious tolerance at St. Finbarr's College. There was tolerance of every economic status. Similarly, there was complete tribal and ethnic harmony at the school because Father Slattery saw to it that everyone accepted everyone else.

As Principal of Saint Finbarr's College from 1956 through 1975, Father Slattery used the threat of being expelled as a deterrent to discourage bad behavior by students. His common warning was "I will send you down that dirt road, and you will never come back, and God is my witness" He, of course, was referring to a one-way journey down the narrow dirt road of Akoka. Saint Finbarr's College campus was the one building in that area of Akoka at that time. It was a long dusty hike from the Unilag Road to the school with heavy bushes on either side of the road.

Father Slattery was a man of small stature. But his heart, energy, and enthusiasm matched those of a giant. He put his energetic temperament into good use in chasing misbehaving students around the school compound. With his robe flowing wildly in the wind, he would take off after boys that he suspected were contravening school rules. It was almost a game of cat and mouse. He monitored the school premises himself. Latecomers and those sneaking out of the school compound during the day hardly escaped his roving eyes. He could run. He could jump. He could even tackle ruffian boys and oh yes, he could really shout. He was a multi-faceted principal; and we all admired, revered, and feared him all at the same time. He also prided himself on being a boxer. Whether he was actually ever a boxer, or whether he put on that bluff to keep us in line, was a frequent debate among the students. When angered, he would challenge the students to a fistfight. Of course, he knew none of us would dare take him on, and he capitalized on that fact. Secondary school kids were much bigger in those days. We had classmates who were in their early twenties. Yet, none was big or man enough to confront the wrath of Father Slattery.

"Father is coming" was a frequently look-out call from boys doing what they were not supposed to be doing. Just like prairie dogs scenting an approaching predator, the boys would run helter-skelter in different directions. There would often be one unfortunate (slower) boy that would be chased down by Father. He would drag the boy into the principal's office for an appropriate punishment. At the next school assembly, we would all hear about the latest mischievous acts of "a few bad boys." I think Father Slattery probably enjoyed those encounters as a way to get his exercise in order to keep fit and trim. He was a nurturing disciplinarian. As strict as he was as a disciplinarian, Father Slattery was also a very forgiving individual. One minute he was shouting and ranting about something, the next minute he was patting you on the back for a good academic or football performance.

How he found the time, resolve, and energy to do all that he did was beyond explanation. Those of us who have tried to emulate his ways can usually be identified by our diverse interests both in avocation and recreation. Father Slattery was a very effervescent man; always excited and animated about everything. There was never a dull moment with him around.

Origin and Background of Rev. Father Denis Joseph Slattery
- Paraphrased from *My Life Story*

Reverend Father Joseph Slattery was born in Fermoy in the County of Cork, South Ireland, on 29th February, 1916, a product of a strong Irish heritage. The Irish are noted for their constant search for self-determination among dominant neighbors. He later became a Catholic priest, founder of Schools, sport administrator, an editor, and a journalist. Father Slattery is a leap-year child. He was always very proud of his leap-year birth date, claiming to be only one-fourth of his actual age. His parents, Mr. Timothy Slattery and Mrs. Kate Slattery (Née Curtin), were blessed with eight children. Denis was the seventh child of the family. Timothy Slattery was a master-cutter and Kate Slattery was a trained dress-maker. They were both from Barrington, Fermoy, a little provincial town in the County of Cork, in the south of Ireland, where the Slattery generations had lived since the 13th century.

The Slattery family was known as "Doers"; a family with a deep sense of adventure, enterprise, and great achievement. The Irish adventurous spirit has remained their greatest contribution to the world. They stride the world in pastoral and political life, breaking new grounds in all spheres.

The American people today remember the Irish among them as the descendants of the builders of Modern America. In 1776, at the signing of the American Constitution, six Irish citizens were signatories to that historic instrument of governance. Timothy Slattery was a disciplinarian, stern, and straight. Kate Slattery was a quiet, serene, and very charitable lady – a combination that was perhaps very necessary for raising eight children, six boys and two girls.

The Slatterys were a family of sportsmen, a trait presumably taken from their father. Timothy Slattery was a great footballer and represented his country as a potential sportsman. His children, particularly Denis, simply carried on the tradition. At a very tender age, Denis J. Slattery was enrolled for his kindergarten education at the Christian Brothers School in Fermoy. He was the only Slattery who did not attend the local Convent school. Young Denis refused to go "to the nuns" at the Presentation Convent. At the Christian Brothers School, the young Slattery was remembered as a wild young man. A healthy kind of wildness, they would say. His activities included *"climbing the highest tree over the River Blackwater and plunging into the deepest depth, searching the woods and forest for birds' nests and eggs, and following the grey hounds on Sunday Soccer."*

He became an Altar boy at the age of ten. He was an excellent liturgist but an average Altar boy. Once an old man who was regular at Mass called him and said, "You serve Mass beautifully. I think you will make a priest." This seemingly harmless remark would come to plant the seed of his vocation. Young Denis had a seriousness of purpose and had often talked about vocations and in due time, he entered the Junior Secondary.

In the Seminary, life was rather drab and hard. Food was poor, dormitories were badly heated, and the chapel was only heated on Sundays. By the second year he had sciatica. He recovered and buried himself deeper into his chosen vocation. He spent two years in the seminary. The extra year was spent getting private tuition in Latin to enable him to pass the Matriculation examination.

The year 1932 marked when Denis Joseph Slattery began his missionary vocation. By 1934, he entered the Novitiate in Clough for a period of two years, and on the 17th December, 1939, he was ordained a priest. He was studious and prayerful at the major Seminary, so he was chosen to go to Rome and study the scriptures in 1940. He was not destined to be in Rome! The 2nd World War broke out and Mussolini shook hands with Hitler, so Rome was out for young Father Denis.

Rev. Father Slattery's first assignment after ordainment was to contribute to raising money for the Church. He felt humiliated because he had to practically beg. Little did he realize that he would be doing the same for the rest of his life. This was the beginning of an arduous and tasking pastoral life. In faraway Lagos, Nigeria, Archbishop Leo Taylor was in dire need of teachers for his diocese. In 1941, the 2nd World War was at its peak. Rev. Fr. Denis Joseph Slattery, 25-year-old Catholic Priest of the Society of African Missions (SMA), was on his way to his posting in Africa. This young Irish priest was part of a growing Irish spiritual empire that included China and the Philippines. The trip was punctuated by a German air attack on the convoy. A German plane had dropped 3 bombs on their ship, which was sailing from Glasgow in a convoy of 50 ships carrying Allied Forces on the Atlantic Ocean. In the tremor following the bombing, the ship rocked violently, dipping from left to right, but did not sink. When they finally sailed into Lagos, the Germans were presumably bombing the Lagos port and ships were not berthing. The ship headed for Port-Harcourt where she berthed. The journey was continued by train from Port-Harcourt to Kaduna to Lagos.

Lagos in 1941 had its fascination for the young Irishman. This is the white man's grave, he wondered. But he did not reckon with Ilawe-Ekiti, a little village in the hinterland of the Western part of Nigeria. Archbishop Taylor was waiting in Lagos. He would welcome the young priest and send him to Ilawe-Ekiti. On his first night at Ilawe-Ekiti, young Fr. Slattery was confronted by a strange pastoral duty. At midnight, a black face had poked its head into the house to ask the Rev. Fr. to come immediately and give blessing to a dying Christian. He performed his duties but the picture remained with him; the black face and the black night.

By the 1940s Archbishop Leo Taylor had built a strong missionary base in the Lagos Diocese. Well-respected and loved by many, Archbishop Taylor was a member of the Society for African Missions (SMA) and of course, the quintessential missionary. He was to recall Rev. Fr. Slattery to Lagos in 1942. By now the young priest he sent to Ilawe-Ekiti now spoke the Yoruba language and could give confession in the language. In Lagos, he was posted to St. Gregory's College, Obalende, as a teacher and games master. His stature seemed to have endeared him to his new students. A mutual relationship was formed which led to great exploits in the football field. The stay at St. Gregory's College was short.

In 1943, he was posted to the Catholic Printing Press as journalist and later Editor of *Catholic Herald.* At the Herald he cultivated a radical posture and became concerned about Nigeria's self-determination as he thundered from the newspaper and the pulpit, "Nigeria for Nigerians." His years as Editor of the Catholic Herald were turbulent. Through the paper, he contributed to the pre-independence struggle, forming a lasting relationship with Labour leaders and politicians. He used the Herald to champion the workers' cause during the General Strike of 1945 and the Enugu Coal Mine strike where 20 striking miners were killed. Thrice, the British Colonial Government tried to throw him out of the country, after several warnings. But according to him he was just doing his duty. ***"The British are gone and I (Slattery) am still here,"*** Slattery would later boast. Fr. Slattery later went on to write his Masters thesis on the labour struggle in Nigeria. A founding member of the Nigerian Union of Journalists (NUJ) and the Guild of Editors, Fr. Slattery contributed immensely to labour and journalism.

Also during these years, he made remarkable contributions to the development of football and football administration in Nigeria. As an inside-left, he had played first division football in Lagos with the Lagos United. But it was as a referee that he made his greatest contribution. His Excellency, Nnamdi Azikiwe, first President of the Federal Republic of Nigeria, was Slattery's linesman in those days. He recalls that he made great strides as a referee probably because he was a Catholic priest; therefore, he was presumed honest. Rev. Fr. Denis Slattery was, at different times, the Chairman of the Referees' Association, Executive member of the Lagos Amateur Football Association, and Chairman of the Nigerian Football Association (N.F.A.)

In 1956, Archbishop Taylor invited Fr. Denis Slattery to establish a secondary school in Lagos. Fr. Slattery saw this assignment as an opportunity to contribute to society as an educationist and a sports administrator. Thus, in January, 1956, he founded St. Finbarr's College as a Technical Grammar School. Classes started on the premises of St. Paul's Primary School, Ebute Metta. St. Finbarr's College became the first school in Nigeria to run in duality a Technical and Grammar School. This was an innovation that endeared the school to parents. Fr. Slattery chose to name the school after Saint Finbarr, who was a great educator, a priest, and a bishop who founded a monastery of prayer and an institution.

In 1960, the school was approved by the Ministry of Education. By this singular action St. Finbarr's College became eligible to participate in the prestigious schoolboys' football competition, the Principal Cup. This had a special thrill for Rev. Fr. Slattery. He had one burning ambition since the day he founded St. Finbarr's College -- to win the prestigious Principal Cup! The name, St. Finbarr's College, was to become synonymous with schoolboy soccer and academic excellence in Nigeria.

Having moved from the premises of St. Paul's Primary School, Ebute Metta to its permanent site in Akoka in 1959, St. Finbarr's College made its debut in the Principal Cup in 1960. They lost to St. Gregory's College that year and in 1961. But in 1962, St. Finbarr's College won the Principal Cup. This was the beginning of unprecedented soccer supremacy in schoolboy football. The college went on to win the Principal Cup for a record nine times. The secret of this success was physical fitness, the provision of necessary training equipment, and a standard pitch (playing field). The myth goes to say that had Fr. Slattery coached the Nigerian national side of those days, they would have won the World Cup. Today, some of his concepts on football administration still remain valid.

Football was the delight of the students of St. Finbarr's; still, Fr. Slattery succeeded in pushing for excellence in other sporting endeavours. In 1960, the College made her debut in the Grier Cup. That year, Eddy Akika of St. Finbarr's College took the coveted Victor Ludorum Trophy winning the Hurdles, Long Jump, and second in the High Jump event.

Slattery ensured that sporting excellence was clearly tied to academic excellence. Through the years and on many occasions, the College had the enviable record of scoring a 100% pass in the WAEC entries. Thus, students of St. Finbarr's were noted for hard work and hard play. Today, Saint Finbarr's College has produced numerous Nigerians who got to the peak of their professional careers and contributed significantly to the development of the Nation. Notable amongst them are: Vice-Admiral Patrick Koshoni (Rtd.), Major-General Cyril Iweze, Nze Mark Odu, Otunba Anthony Olusegun Odugbesan, Dr. J. A. Ikem, Dr. Segun Ogundimu, Chief Empire Kanu P, Professor Steve Elesha, Dr. Tayo Shokunbi, Airvice Marshal Wilfred Ozah, Tom Borha, Segun Ajanlekoko.

Father Denis Slattery retired from St. Finbarr's College in 1975. He returned to his first love, his pastoral duties. So, to St. Denis Catholic Church, Bariga he retired; to a total service to the Church as Parish priest. He eventually retired as Vicar-General to the Archdiocese of Lagos, and left his footprints again, in the sand of time. Rev. Fr. Denis J. Slattery is a true Nigerian patriot of Irish parentage, who contributed to the pioneering of technical education in secondary schools and the growth of football administration in Nigeria. Rev. Fr. D. J. Slattery was a Missionary, Educationist, Journalist, Technocrat, Football Administrator, a mentor of sports, and one of nature's exceptional gentlemen.

Selected Quotes from Father Slattery's Book, *My Life Story*, **are presented in the Appendix to this book. Rev. Father Slattery was an outstanding example of the Irish Catholic Missionary movement, which in this century saw many thousands of Irish Reverend Fathers and Sisters leave Ireland to take the Christian message to the four corners of the world. He dedicated 56 years of his earthly life to the development of the Nigerian humanity. A keen sportsman and Journalist, he served Nigeria in many capacities including Chairmanship of the Nigerian Football Association (NFA). He also edited the Catholic Herald Newspaper for many years. He brought with him from Ireland, a keen appreciation of the value of education, without which freedom, responsibility, or development is impossible.**

In his great desire to inform, Father Slattery became actively involved in the development of Journalism and Education. His major contribution to education, St. Finbarr's College, Akoka, is named after Saint Finbarr – the patron saint of his native county of Cork. His other enduring legacy to Nigeria, football, comes from his own passionate love of sport. Here, he obviously tapped into a rich vein in Nigerian life – a truly fanatical love of football. A list of his achievements and contributions is presented below.

Slattery's Achievements and Contributions

1. Vice-Chairman of the Society for the Bribe Scorners
2. Assistant Honorary Secretary of the Nigerian Olympic & British Empire Games Association
3. Publicity Secretary of the Lagos District Amateur Football Association
4. Member of the Council of African Students in North America
5. Assistant Secretary of the Nigerian Football Association
6. Honorary Secretary of the Commonwealth Games Appeal Fund
7. Catholic Representative of the Broadcasting Services (Religious)
8. Chairman of the Nigerian Referees Association
9. Chairman of the Council of Social Workers (Boy Scouts, Catholic Youth Organization, Salvation Army, Boys' Brigade, Y.M.C.A., Colony Welfare Organizations, Girls Guide, and Youth Clubs)
10. Chairman of the Leper Colony of Nigeria
11. Chairman of the Nigerian Football Association (NFA)
12. Editor of the Catholic Herald (Newspaper)
13. Foundation Member of the Nigerian Union of Journalists
14. Member of the Nigerian Guild of Editors
15. Founder and Principal of St. Finbarr's College, Akoka, Lagos
16. Founder of SS Peter & Paul, Shomolu
17. Founder of Our Lady of Fatima Private School, Bariga

18. Founder of St. Joseph's Vocational School, Akoka
19. Coordinator of the T.I.M.E. Project, Akoka
20. Founder of St. Finbarr's Catholic Church, Akoka, Lagos
21. Founder of St. Gabriel's Catholic Church
22. Founder of St. Flavius Catholic Church, Oworonshoki
23. Parish Priest of St. Denis Catholic Church
24. Vicar-General of the Catholic Church of Nigeria – Lagos Archdiocese (Rtd.)

Chapter Four
The Story of Saint Finbarr's College

The history of Saint Finbarr's College is a favorite pastime of all the former and present students of the school. Saint Finbarr's College is most noted for three characteristics:

1. Academics
2. Football
3. Discipline

Rev. Father D.J. Slattery came to Nigeria in 1939, and having served in a parish in the Yoruba Inland Town in the Old Western Region, was posted to St. Gregory's College Obalende as a teacher and later became the Games Master. He later became the editor of the Catholic Herald in Mushin. It was during this period that the thought of establishing a unique school occurred to him. His school became the first bilateral school in the country, combining full Grammar (called Basic) with Arts and Technical subjects. In the 1955/56 academic year, with six students, fondly referred to as "the first six", a new school, but without a name, was born.

The new school had no address and had to be accommodated in the newly built St. Paul's Catholic Primary School, Apapa

Road. The next task was to look for a site for the new school. Rev. Father D. J. Slattery, after an eleven-month search, which took him through the then jungles of Apapa, and now the present National Stadium, eventually got to another jungle in Akoka where he met a man who knew him but he did not know the man. The friendly disposition of the man made it easy for him to acquire a twenty-plot piece of land in the present site of the school. In 1959, the school moved from Apapa Road to its present site in Akoka, and in 1963, the school was officially opened by Dr. Nnandi Azikiwe, the first President of Nigeria, who was a personal friend of Fr. Slattery.

In a tactical move, he got a grant from the then British Colonial Government, with which he set up a ten-classroom block, two technical drawing rooms, a technical block, an administrative block, which also houses the teachers staff room, and a dining room assembly hall with a well equipped kitchen. Among the first teachers of the school were the late Chief Albert Bankole, Fr. Slattery himself, and Mr. F. Ekpeti.

The school made its first attempt at the West African School Certificate Examinations in 1961, having been approved in 1960. In that first attempt, the technical department had 100% passes, with 80% making 3 or 4 credits, while the Grammar, or basic as they were called, had 50% passes with two of them making distinctions. These boys were also tops in sports and Vice-Admiral Patrick Koshoni (Rtd) happens to be one of the two. From then on the result kept improving year after year, with the technical department consistently recording 100% passes. In fact, in those days of Grade 1, Grade 2, and Grade 3 categorization of WAEC results, whenever the result was released, the understanding or common expectation was that all candidates would normally pass and what everybody was interested in was how many came out in Grade One or Grade Two: Grade Three was regarded as a consolation result. This trend remained true until the government takeover of schools in the mid 1970's.

Exploits In Sports

Rev. Father Denis J. Slattery, being a Games Master and an International Referee, was very eager to put the school at the forefront quickly in football since it would take 5 years for the school to prove its excellence in academics. In its first year of existence, it pitched itself in a football match against its host Primary School, St. Paul's Primary School, Apapa Road and lost 1-2. In 1957, it faced much older St. Gregory's "Rabbits," where Father Slattery himself had been a Games Master. The school later had a number of matches with another older School, the Ahmadiya College, Agege. It was a very ambitious venture for the school, in its first four years of existence on 3rd June 1960, to make its first attempt on the Zard Cup, a nationwide inter Secondary School competition, which later became the Principals Cup. The school again lost to its counterpart institution, St. Gregory's College, 1-3. In 1961 it met the school again and lost 0-1 after an initial draw of 2-2, and won the Principals Cup for the first time in 1962, six years after its inception. This victory was repeated in 1966, 1968, and 1969. From then St. Finbarr's College team became a team to beat. Weaker teams feared any match with St. Finbarr's while stronger ones like C.M.S. Grammar School, Baptist Academy, Igbobi College, and of course, the big brother St. Gregory's, always looked forward to a tough encounter. In 1971, 1972, and 1973, the school had the Principals Cup, having won it 3 consecutive times.

It is noteworthy that in the 1970's and 1980's the school produced international players like Thompson Oliha, Nduka Ugbade, Samson SiaSia, and Henry Nwosu, just to mention a few. In fact in those days, for any candidate to aspire to come to St. Finbarr's, he must be academically sound and/or physically superior in football. Stephen Keshi, who is presently the coach of Togo's National Football team, captained Finbarr's Football team. He later went on to captain and coach Nigeria's national team.

Rev. Father Denis J. Slattery placed a very high premium on discipline and could expel any student even if he was the best in academics or in football, once it was established that he had committed a serious offense. The gate used to be referred to as the gate of no return. There was no point in appealing a case of expulsion. Father Slattery never entertained such acts – no pleading, no begging, and no beseeching. Saint Finbarr's College had four commandments, which constitute the Moral Pillars of the school.

1. Any student caught stealing will be expelled.
2. Any student caught copying during an examination time will be expelled.
3. Any student caught leaving the school compound during school hours without the Principal's permission will be expelled.
4. Any student caught smoking or with drugs will be expelled.

By the early 1970's Rev. Fr. D. J. Slattery had a vision of making St. Finbarr's College all encompassing in technical studies. He, therefore, decided to expand the technical workshops to cater both for the Senior and Junior Student. He introduced auto mechanics, electrical, and electronics departments. Two modern technical workshops were built from grants raised by his friends and overseas associates. The workshops were completed and fully equipped. They had hardly been used for two years when the government took over private schools. From 1976, the ideals for which St. Finbarr's stood started suffering a serious decline. The school became over-populated, indiscipline crept in and reached a frightening stage in the second half of the 1990's.

However, a new lease on life started returning to the school, following the return of the schools by the government on the 2nd of October, 2001. The return took effect in 2003. A great purge started and many of the students who could not adjust were dismissed while those who could not stand the changes withdrew voluntarily. Consequently, by 2005, the enrolment at the school has gone down to a manageable level of 658 with the inherited "government students" constituting 413 students of the population. Since inception, to the present administration, St. Finbarr's College has had 6 principals:

1. Very Rev. Father D. J. Slattery
   Founding Principal   1955-1975
2. Late Anthony Onoera 1975-1976
3. Mr. A. A. Kpotie   1977-1998
4. Mr. Joseph Adusse   1998-2001
5. Mr. C. B. Adejoya, October 2001 to December 2003
6. Mr. Daniel Ikediobi, January 2004 - Present

The school is now managed by an administrator from the Catholic Mission, Rev. Fr. J. G. Oduntan.

Chapter Five
Fond Memories of Saint
Finbarr's College

My life has been intimately intertwined with events associated with Saint Finbarr's College. My life then and my life now still bear remarkable allegiance to some memorable events during my days at the school. I had many good times at Saint Finbarr's College.

Starting at Saint Finbarr's College was not easy at first. Since I had to start classes the very next day after I was miraculously admitted, I was totally unprepared. I had no uniform, still no school shoes, and no books. My sister, the late Mrs. Durosimi (Mrs. Shojobi at that time) had generously agreed to pay my school fees. But the arrangement was for my mother to pay for my books, uniforms, and other essential items. Therein lay the initial obstacles. My mother was not immediately prepared for such responsibilities. She was a petty trader, plying her migrant trade between Ondo Township, Atijere, Okitipupa, Ejinrin, and Epe. She was so overjoyed that I had gained admission into a secondary school that she pledged to sell her prized jewelries and family heirlooms to raise the money needed to carry out her own end of the bargain. But, selling those things required some time. So, there was a time lag between when I had to start classes and when my mother could buy my uniforms, shoes, and books.

Father Slattery allowed me to attend classes for one whole week without uniform before sending me home. This was an unmistakable message that I needed to get my school uniform by hook or crook. Somehow my mother was able to come up with the money for my uniform. As for the books, Father Slattery allowed me to borrow some books from the school library. Gradually, I settled into the business of my secondary school education.

Immaculate Conception Question

Although Father Slattery knew me personally at that time because of the way I entered the school, but what really brought us close together was a miscue that I committed in his religious studies class. In one of the early examination questions that I faced in his class, I missed the definition of immaculate conception. What I presented as the definition was the exact opposite of the answer. The error must have been due to my lack of knowledge or a temporary gap in my train of thought. I can't quite explain how the error occurred. But the result was that Father Slattery was very furious. He said I had committed blasphemy. "Son, you have sinned. The thing you should have done was to not write anything if you knew you did not know the answer," he exclaimed. "I will have to pray for you." I believed he made such a big deal of the issue not just because of the error itself, but because he wanted to make sure that I got the message. And yes, indeed, I got the message. That incident encouraged me to never let any point of religious studies slide through my fingers again. Thereafter, I became one of the best students in Father Slattery's classes. This is an example of how Father Slattery used shrewd antics to get the attention of students. It was a clever mind game that he played to get students to perform at their best.

Discipline at Saint Finbarr's College

Discipline was and still is a major attribute and attraction of Saint Finbarr's College. Parents take delight in the discipline that kids get at the school. The mantra of the school revolve around three tenets of:

1. Academics
2. Football
3. Discipline

The school was widely noted for these. Father Slattery provided the educational infrastructure to pursue academics. He also provided the sports environment to ensure the accomplishment of an esteemed football prowess. Finally, he conjured the physical presence to impose discipline on everyone. There was a rule for everything. Abiding by those rules helped in shaping the future outlook of the students.

Fun With BB Cartoons

Cartoon experiments in the Art Room of Saint Finbarrs led to a brief opportunity to draw cartoon strips for the Children's Page of Daily Times in 1970 and 1971. The art teacher and Father Slattery were very proud of this "educational outreach" as they called it because I had a contract and got paid for the cartoons that were published in the newspaper. This was a big accomplishment for a high school kid in those days. Father Slattery was particularly impressed because the school was still relatively young and needed to build a good reputation in other areas apart from football. So, he would widely commend and publicize any outside accomplishments of students of the school.

Mosquito and Rabbit Football Teams

While I was at Saint Finbarr's, I played on the mosquito and rabbit football teams. These were the junior level teams designed to prepare boys for the full-fledged first-eleven team later on. My self-proclaimed nickname for playing football was "Iron Pillar." Some of my fun-loving classmates (notably Benedict Ikwenobe) translated the nickname into different variations. These invoked a lot of fun and laughter whenever we were on a playing field. Although I was a decent player, I was never committed to being on the regular team of Saint Finbarr's College. Late Mr. Anthony Onoera (former principal), while coaching our rabbit team, lamented that if I would fully commit to playing football, I could be a superb Finbarr's player. Of course, the competition for securing a spot on the regular team was incredibly keen and I wasn't fully committed to training to be a regular soccer player. Saint Finbarr's College football players were of a different stock – highly skilled and talented. Many of them, even in high school, could have played on professional teams. In fact, the 1970 team was so good that there was a plan to have the team play the professional team Stationery Stores. But the untimely death of Chief Israel Adebajo, the owner of Stationery Stores, just one day before the scheduled match, scuttled the plan. So, we never got to find out if our high school team could have beaten a full-fledged professional team. In my later years, recalling my Saint Finbarr's soccer heritage, I did blossom into a more respectable recreational player. I played on my university team in Tennessee and later on adult recreational teams in Florida and Oklahoma.

Inter-House Sports

Inter-house sports were another big part of the experience at Saint Finbarr's College. Although I participated in several sports at the school, I was always only on the fringes of excellence in each one. My primary goal was more to be a part of the fun of sports. I don't recall devoting the necessary training time needed to excel. But I occasionally used the pretext of going for sports training at the school to escape from home so that I could go and play elsewhere. My sister always gave me permission to go out if I connected the reason to some sports activity at the school. She knew sports was very important at Saint Finbarr's and she never wanted to interfere with the school's expectations.

Sneaking Off-Campus

Following my enrollment at Saint Finbarr's College, I occasionally stayed with my sister at the Unilag Staff Quarters. Whenever she did not have a house help, I would move in with her to provide household support covering all manners of household chores including kitchen service and gardening. My present affinity for the kitchen and household chores was shaped in those years. Living so close to the college often created temptations for us to sneak out of school during school hours. This was a no-no according to the rules of the school. But young boys always enjoy the challenge (and perils) of doing what they are told not to do. If we managed to sneak out without being caught by Father Slattery, we would visit the homes of classmates living at Akoka and make the long trek to Lagoon at the edge of Unilag campus – in search of fun and play. Thinking back now, it was a big risk. I can never explain why we would have risked being permanently expelled from the school. Whenever we successfully got out and back to the school compound, we would feel a sense of great accomplishment. With that euphoria, we would start looking forward to the next opportunity to sneak out again. I thank God that no one in my group of friends was ever caught engaging in this mischievous act. Boys that were caught faced the full wrath of Father Slattery.

Deji Badiru and classmates in Physics Lab (1971)

(L-R: Michael Elumeze, Deji Badiru, Joseph Malokwu)

Class III A (1970)

Deji Badiru (middle) and classmates

Chapter Six
Life After Finbarr's College

By the time I left Saint Finbarr's College in December 1972, my fun days of Lagos were slowing ebbing. 1970 represented the height of my enjoyment of Lagos streets. Starting in 1973, several other things were beginning to creep into my life. I still wanted to continue my association with my neighbourhood friends. I belonged to informal clubs dedicated to having fun in the neighbourhoods. There was the Lagos Island Rascals and there was The Kano Street Gang at Ebute Metta. In 1966, I had lived with my uncle at Bamgbose Street right across from Campus Square. I made several friends on the tough playgrounds of campus square. In my various living arrangements with relatives between 1961 and 1972, I had resided at various locations in the Lagos Metropolis. I had lived at Andrew Street, Lagos; Tokunboh Street, Lagos; Bamgbose Street, Lagos; Ita Alagba Street, Lagos; Kano Street, Ebute Metta; Brickfield Road, Ebute Metta; Bode Thomas Street, Surulere; and University of Lagos Staff Quarters.

Even after finishing secondary school, I still enjoyed cruising many of the fun neighbourhoods of my previous habitats. My family started to worry about my future. They were concerned that I was nonchalant and indifferent about my future. They deplored my interest in attending parties in Lagos. They wanted me to aggressively start seeking admission to a university. But I would always defend myself by claiming that I knew "what I was doing." I maintained that I had everything under control. Underneath the party image, I had a structured and determined mind focused on being successful with whatever I wanted to do. Father Slattery had impacted the discipline of success on all his students; and I was sure I was not going to end up destitute. My attitude was "Let me enjoy myself for now; success is destined to come later on."

Chapter Seven
The Blessing of Meeting My Wife

That I met and married my wife was due to an act of coincidence that had its roots in the Art Room of Saint Finbarr's College. Had I not attended Saint Finbarr's College; had I not been in the school's art room painting a colorful rooster; had I not been in good favour with the art teacher; had the art teacher not given me a job referral to Mr. Nupo Samuel at the Lagos State Ministry of Education – Audio Visual Aids Section; had I not returned to the painting of the colorful rooster; I would not have my wife of today. It was a step-wise progression from Saint Finbarr's College art room to the eventual liaison with my future wife.

I was a good student of Art and our art teacher took a special interest in my future professional outlook. He felt that I was good enough to become a renowned professional artist. Being somewhat of an all-rounder, each of my other teachers had expressed similar expectations that I would go into a profession fitting his or her own subject. The French teacher, Mr. Akinrimade, expected me to become a professional in the Nigerian foreign mission with assignments to French-speaking countries. He later tried to get me to attend the

Nigerian Defense Academy (NDA), thinking that I would make a great Army officer in Nigeria's missions in the African Francophone countries. The Biology teacher, Mr. A. A. Kpotie, who later became Principal, advised that I should go into the medical field. The English teacher hoped that I would follow his profession and become an English teacher, or a writer, or a poet. The Physics teacher suggested that I would make an excellent scientist. My Mathematics teacher wanted me to become an engineer. Observing my later performance in his own Religious Studies class, Father himself thought I would be a good religious ambassador, bridging the division between Christians and Moslems. As for me, I just went with the flow. I did not pay much attention to what the future held for me in terms of a profession. I believed in existentialism and adapted to whatever came up for the moment. Enjoying the moment was all that mattered to me.

In the Art room, I experimented with various drawing and painting exercises. It was in preparation for my Art School Certificate examination that I came across the painting of animals. The painting of one particular colourful rooster (cock) attracted my attention for several weeks. I never completed the painting to my own level of satisfaction. So, I abandoned the project. This was around the middle of 1972. A couple of years later, it turned out that a return to the painting of a colourful rooster would seal my fate with my future wife.

Two weeks after finishing my School Certificate examination I secured a job as a factory supervisor at Associated Industries Limited (AIL) in Ikeja. My School Cert results had not come out by that time. So, I did not know what direction I was going to pursue either in terms of further studies or long-term employment. I was on night shift at AIL, starting work around 3p.m. and closing at 11p.m. I never enjoyed the work at all, even though the salary was very good by the standards of the day. I longed for a "more regular" job schedule, where I would close around 4 p.m. and I could spend the afternoons and evenings with my neighbourhood friends. So, I abruptly left AIL after only three weeks. My next employment was at UTC as an Accounts Clerk at the Broad Street location of the company. I did well at this job, but the work schedule was too oppressive for a freshly-liberated high school graduate whose primary interest was having afternoon fun in the neighbourhood. As an Accounts Clerk, I was required to work overtime sometimes in the evenings and weekends. This did not suit me well. So, I left UTC after two months although I had no immediate prospects for another employment. Unemployed, I roamed the streets of Lagos as I had been accustomed to in search of new friendships and fun opportunities. I greatly enjoyed the freedom and lack of worries of those days. I enjoyed the freedom to roam the city. Even nowadays, I still enjoy my hands-on and legs-on approach to duties. "Legs-on" means that I like going places to get things done directly myself. This direct approach is a good way to ensure efficiency and effectiveness of actions.

By March 1973, the School Cert results were out and Father Slattery had personally sent someone to my residence at 13 Brickfield Road, Apapa Road to proudly announce that I came out with Grade I Distinction in the School Cert. This energized me to want to drop my unemployment status. So, I went back to the job market in search of re-employment. Heartened by my School Cert results, I was not concerned about not being successful in the job market. My most cherished results were a "1" in English, a "1" in French, a "2" in Mathematics, and a "2" in Art. Although I did well in all my subjects, these were my four favorite and preferred subjects.

My former Art teacher at Saint Finbarr's College came to know of how well I had performed in the School Certificate Art examination and decided that he must get me into the art profession. He sent a message to me at home to inform me that the Lagos State Ministry of Education's Audio Visual Aids

Section on Broad Street was in need of a graphics artist. He referred me to a friend of his, Mr. S. Nupo Samuel, who was a senior staff in charge of the Art Unit. Mr. Samuel received his BSc in Fine Art from Ahmadu Bello University. He would later encourage me to seek admission for Fine Art at the same university. I spent several weeks doing gratis drawing for Mr. Samuel in anticipation of an appropriate job opening in the Art Unit. He implored me to be patient. He had to find the right time and occasion to introduce me to his boss, the head of the Audio Visual Aids Section. The Section Head at that time was Mrs. F. R. A. Thanni. She had informed Mr. Samuel that the section did not have any Graphic Arts position even though Mr. Samuel urgently needed an assistant. But after several weeks of drawing for the Section free of charge, Mrs. Thanni decided, upon becoming aware of my School Cert results, that she could get me into the Ministry as a Clerical Officer. That was how I started as a Clerical Officer in the Lagos State Ministry of Education in April 1973. I was immediately posted to the Audio Visual Aids Section. Although my official title was Clerical Officer, my actual duties were as a graphic artist. I drew pictures that accompanied English language captions for children's television programs. The programs were designed to introduce children to the English Language. If a caption said, "This is a dog," I would draw a dog to depict the context. It was a fun and rewarding job. The work load was very low because we broadcast the programs only once a week. So, in between official drawing assignments, I would engage in casual drawing and painting.

In December 1973, Miss Iswat Kuforiji, was employed in the same Audio Visual Aids Section. I immediately set my eyes on her as my future wife. I was only 21 and she was only 17. But I was undeterred by our youthful ages. She was very beautiful and unattached. She had just moved to Lagos from Ilaro. I was determined to snatch her before she could fall into the hands of Lagos boys with roving eyes. I had been one of those boys. So, I knew I had to move fast to protect her from the likes of me. I began to direct all my attention and energy to convincing her that I was the designated person for her. Unfortunately, all my attempts to woo her were futile. She clearly hated my guts. She detested my Lagos-boy arrogance. The air of city sophistication that I had tried to use to impress her actually turned her against me. She would have nothing to do with me. Even my proud Saint Finbarr's College roots could not immediately do the trick. The Boys of Saint Finbarr's College in those days believed in and used the aura of Saint Finbarr's College to get girls. Many high-school girls in Lagos at that time were anxious to fall for a Finbarr's boy. But this girl, coming from the relatively rural setting of Ilaro, was not aware of the Saint Finbarr's College aura. So, she was not impressed. I decided to give her up because, frankly, there were other old fishes already in the catch. I was on the verge of telling her off when my Saint Finbarr's College origin came into place in a very unexpected way.

Since she was not responding, I had redirected my attention once again to my casual drawings and paintings in the office. I returned to the painting of the colourful rooster that I had abandoned in the Saint Finbarr's College Art Room several months earlier. One day, I was seriously engrossed in painting the rooster when Iswat came beside me to ask what I was painting. A stroke of ingenuity struck me right then. Without time to think of a cute response, I blurted out "This colourful rooster that I am painting represents me; and right here beside him I am going to paint a hen; and that hen will represent you." Well, that did the trick. She was completely disarmed. All she could mutter was, "Okay." And that was how we embarked on our journey of dating and eventually getting married in 1975. September 25, 2005 will mark our thirtieth wedding anniversary. To this date, that painting of the rooster and the hen has remained a constant feature of decoration in my offices. The painting is presently proudly displayed in my office at the University of Tennessee. A photograph of it can be found in my painting gallery. What a blessing!

Family Blessings

Meeting Iswat was what purged me of the Lagos street demons that were plaguing me. If I had not met her at that time, my care-free, fun-loving, and reckless partying around Lagos could have derailed my professional future. I was a good dancer with incredible staying stamina on the dance floor. So, I was frequently sought after at Lagos party events as a "life of the party." You might say I was fooloose and fancy free. That reputation was what led to the objection of Iswat's sister, Alhaja R. Omosanya, when she found out that I was dating her sister. She cautioned, "That boy has a popular reputation among the Broad Street and Ministry girls. You should stay away from him. He would use you and dump you." This was an erroneous and undeserved reputation. I was popular for my party dancing, but I actually did not have many girl friends. In fact, I had no girl friend at all when I met Iswat. I was spending so much time on the dance floors that I did not devote sufficient time to wooing a girl. Seeing how girls were anxious to dance with me at parties, some people concluded erroneously that I must be dating several girls. I wish I was; but that was not the case.

On the dance floor, I was transformed into a different person, possessed by the rhythms of good music, any type of music at all. I rarely ate or drank at parties. My entire focus was always on my dance steps. I was always a spectacle to watch at Lagos parties of those days. My interest in permanently preserving my dancing repertoire led to my creating my "Dancing Professor" videotape later on in the USA. That video never saw any level of distribution because my wife found it embarrassing and thought it did not befit my other reputation as a learned professional. I still covertly keep a few copies of the video tape and I sneak them out of the house every now and then to show to my friends, if they promise not to tell my wife that they have seen the tape.

When I found out about Alhaja's objection to my dating Iswat, I decided to confront her boldly. I invited her to lunch. It was like reaching out with impunity to a revered elder. What an insult! Iswat was scared because Alhaja was a no-nonsense stern sister. Iswat thought Alhaja would never grant me an audience. But I approached Alhaja with my usual calm and calculated demeanor. Surprisingly, and much to Iswat's adoration of my skills of approach, Alhaja agreed to meet with me. I believe she was impressed with my boldness and frankness in the issue at hand. Boys of that age and involved in such abominable act of dating innocent girls dared not show their faces to the girl's family. But here I was, only 22 years old (in 1974), embarking on a journey normally reserved for the elders of a family. Alhaja was impressed with my grown-up attitude. So, she was interested in whatever I had to say. We had a nice conversation over lunch at one of popular canteens next to the Broad Street Headquarters of the Lagos State Ministry of Education, where she was working at that time. Alhaja worked at the Ministry Headquarters while Iswat and I worked at the Audio Visual Aids Section of the Ministry, also on Broad Street, but several kilometers eastward. Without trying to be defensive, I told Alhaja that all she had heard about me from the Ministry girls was true (there was no point trying to convince her otherwise); but that I was ready to settle down. Now that I had found the right person for me, I would no longer engage in partying and search around Lagos. Alhaja bought my pledge. She then gave her blessings to the relationship. But she warned that Iswat's parents would be hard to convince. After all, they had just sent her to Lagos for a better life, not to be quickly swept up into an uncertain marital future. I told Alhaja not to worry. I would travel to Ilaro to speak with Iswat's parents. Alhaja was aghast. She counseled me that that was a mission for the elders of the family. I could not possibly serve as my own emissary to my bride's parents. You see, I had the confidence and naivety of an uninitiated young man. So, I was not going to be encumbered by the usual tradition. I convinced Alhaja to let me make the trip to Ilaro. But she insisted that she would have to accompany me. So, we set a conducive date to travel to Ilaro. But before the scheduled date, Iswat's mother happened to travel to Lagos.

I suspected that she must have got a hint of what was afoot and wanted to come to Lagos to dissuade us. I remember clearly the day she showed up unexpectedly in our office. Iswat almost melted with fright. She had earlier warned me that her mother was tough and might not approve of me. Previous family history dictated that concern. There was a medical doctor that had wanted to marry Alhaja in her spinster days. The dreams of the suitor fell flat when he was not approved by the mother the very first time she laid her eyes on him. Alhaja was very beautiful (and still is) and several suitors had approached her to no avail on account of the mother's objection. So, Iswat did not hold much hope for our relationship. But, as usual, I told her to let me handle the matter. She wanted me to hide so that I would not have to confront her mother. Once she objected, there would be no recourse. But I would have none of the hiding suggestion. I had never hidden from anyone, again capitalizing on my Lagos brashness. I decided to meet and greet Mama. Mama's heart softened instantly as soon as I greeted her. There was nothing special about my physical looks that could have impressed her. But my manner of approach, candor, and boldness indicated that I had nothing to hide. So, instead of her mounting an objection, she became a supportive ally to the scheme. Alhaja, Mama, and I then set out to plot how we would approach Papa at Ilaro. Iswat was kept out of the background scheming. She would always wait anxiously for me to brief her on the covert discussions with her sister and mother. As the proceedings went on, she became increasingly confident in my ability to accomplish the enormous task. All the fears she had been nursing became non-issues once I got into handling them. That incipient faith that she developed in me at that time still rules our relationship until this day. She completely entrusted her life to me at that time. She was very trusting. She thought I could do anything. It is that huge responsibility that has kept me on the straight and narrow path all these years. I never wanted to let her down or disappoint her in whatever she expected of me.

Well, the day to travel to meet Papa eventually came. Iswat waited nervously in Lagos. There were hush-hush whisperings in Papa's household on Leslie Road, Ilaro, as Alhaja and I arrived. No one knew what was going to happen. Contrary to all the disturbing speculations, Papa received me exceedingly well. It was one of the most exhilarating experiences of my life. Papa Kuforiji was a very educated man. That impressed me a lot because I was confident that I could communicate with him on logical basis without too much of the local sentiments common in illiterate in-laws of those days. He had been a soldier in World War II and had traveled extensively. Although he was retired at that time, he was still professionally popular in the town. With a very rational discussion and without hesitation, he gave his blessings. But one issue that gave him concern was the fact that I came alone without a representative from my own family members. But in a way, he commended my bravery and maturity in wanting to pave the way for family-to-family discussions later on. He insisted that I must inform my own family and bring them to a larger meeting at a later date. Thus, my fate with Iswat was sealed. We subsequently got married on September 25, 1975. I was barely 23, just three weeks after my 22nd birthday; and she was 19, exactly three months shy of her twentieth birthday. More blessings than I can count.

Many of my family members are still amazed at how quickly and completely I settled down after meeting Iswat. There were internal speculations that she must have used some local "juju" medicine from Ilaro to calm me down and purge the party demons. But what actually captured and transformed me was her captivating beauty. I had no reason to look anywhere else.

I thank Saint Finbarr's College for creating the pathway to meeting my beautiful and faithful wife. It was through Saint Finbarr's College that I met my art teacher. It was through the art teacher that I met Mr. Nupo Samuel. It was through Mr. Samuel that I ended up at the Audio Visual Aids Section of the Lagos State Ministry of Education. It was through that work place that Iswat walked into my life. It was the painting exercise that started at Saint Finbarr's Art Room that finally softened Iswat's heart towards me. If not for Saint Finbarr's College, I would not have met her, at least not in the context that eventually united us as husband and wife.

Chapter Eight
Academic and Professional Pursuits

The blessings of Saint Finbarr's College continued to follow me into the years beyond high school. While I was still working at Lagos State Ministry of Education, I came across an advertisement for clerks at Central Bank of Nigeria (CBN). I applied and was fortunate to secure employment as Clerk Grade C. I was posted to the Staff Pay Office. I joined CBN in April 1974. Iswat was still working at the ministry. But CBN was a short trekking distance from the ministry. So, we did not feel physically disconnected. It was at Central Ban that I met Mr. Supo Adedeji, who later became a close friend and a selfless helper in my pursuits of overseas scholarships later on. I was not thinking of an immediate departure for overseas studies because I had Iswat to think of.

Central Bank was conducting a certificate review of all staff sometime late in 1974. That was when several senior administrators came in contact with my school cert results. I was summoned to the office of Alhaji Elias, who was then a department head. He chastised me for not putting my high school performance to good use. He felt such a school cert result should be leveraged to pursue further studies overseas.

I told him I was planning to go abroad for further studies, but I had not saved enough money yet. My family members were already concerned that I was whiling away my post-secondary schools. It was suspected that I was getting carried away with the fun life of Lagos and was not interested in furthering my education. Alhaji Elias' concern only served to confirm the fears of my family. He insisted that I must apply for scholarships to facilitate my further studies forthwith. When I subsequently secured Federal Government scholarships, he willingly served as one of my guarantors. Other individuals serving as my guarantors for the scholarship offers were Mr. Nupo Samuel and my brother, the Late Mr. Atanda Badiru. Father Slattery continued to provide written testimonials as required for many of my scholarship and university admission processes. Such was his dedication to the welfare and success of his students that he always found the time to provide written recommendations.

In December 1975, I proceeded to the USA to start my studies in Industrial Engineering at Tennessee Technological University. I was on a full scholarship from the Federal Government of Nigeria. Iswat came to join me in the USA in June 1976. So began my academic and professional pursuits in the USA.

1984 Reunion with Father Slattery

In Summer 1984, I visited Nigeria for the first time in eight years.; my first visit home after going to the USA in December1975. It was during that visit that my sister reunited me with Father Slattery. She was very proud of my academic achievement in the USA and wanted Father Slattery to be aware of what I had accomplished so far. We visited Father Slattery at his Akoka home. He had been displaced as the principal of the Saint Finbarr's College by that time. It was a very sad feeling for me to see him not on the school compound, but in a secluded house. No longer was he engaged in doing what he loved most – running Saint Finbarr's College. He recounted how bored he was for not being involved in school affairs. But at the same time, he was grateful that he then had time to devote more energy to the Church.

During the visit, Father Slattery instructed me to consolidate whatever I was planning to do on behalf of SFCOBA with what Segun was already doing. He was full of praise for Segun and his exceptional leadership skills. Since that time, Segun and I have worked closely with other dedicated Finbarrians to advance the cause of SFCOBA and the school.

I entered the academic career primarily because of my interest in following the educational lineage established by Reverend Father Slattery.

Later on, as Dean of University College at the University of Oklahoma, I tried my best to help students, foreigners and Americans alike, with their educational objectives. This created an immense gratification for me. One enters the teaching profession, not because of the financial rewards possible, but because of the opportunity to impart knowledge to others. "Teach onto others as you have been taught" is my premise for teaching. I have continued this same philosophy in my present professorial position at the University of Tennessee.

Equation of Success

Recalling the discipline impacted by my years at Saint Finbarr's College, I created what I called the equation of success for my students. The axiom, referred to as "Badiru's Equations of Success," entreats students to rely more on their self-discipline in accomplishing goals and objectives. The equation says that success is a function of three primarily factors: raw intelligence, common sense, and self-discipline.

$$S = f(x, y, z),$$

Deji Badiru

Where:

x = Intelligence, which is an innate attribute, which every one of us is endowed with.

y = Common sense, which is an acquired trait from our everyday social interactions.

z = Self-Discipline, which is an inner drive (personal control), which helps an individual to blend common sense with intelligence in order to achieve success.

With this equation, success is within everyone's control. One cannot succeed on intelligence alone. Common sense and self-discipline must be used to facilitate success.

Chapter Nine
Induction as a Conqueror

On October 1, 1998, several Old Boys and I were inducted into the esteemed order of "Distinguished Conqueror (DC)" of Saint Finbarr's College, an exalted position of recognition for Finbarr's Alumni. Friends and family members accompanied me to the event at Sheraton Hotel. The installation accompanied the establishment of the annual distinguished lecture series, which took place on October 7, 1998. Prof. Awele Maduemezia was the main inaugural speaker. Father Slattery's speech delivered at the inaugural lecture typified his life-long service to Nigeria. He was in Ireland at the time and could not deliver the speech in person. But the power of the words contained in the prepared speech represented him so very well, as if he was there in person.

Speech by Rev. Father Slattery – October 7, 1998

"Welcome to all – distinguished lecturer, parents, audience and students.

Many months ago, the President of St. Finbarr's, Segun Ajanlekoko, told me that the Executive Committee of the

Finbarr's Old Boys were planning on inaugurating an annual distinguished guest lecture. To be truthful, I pooh-poohed the whole idea. I asked myself how a comparatively young College could launch such an august event in a city like Lagos, where there are many educational colleges and universities of great distinction.

Is St. Finbarr's going to be the first college to honour their first Principal? Why?

The more I thought about it, the more I realized that the proposed lecturer of today has launched, I am sure, many First Lectures before now. But it occurs to me that it is the first time that a secondary school Principal was to be honoured by past pupils in this way.

Today's Guest Speaker is Professor Awele Maduemezia, the former Vice-Chancellor of Edo State University, Ekpoma. Our speaker today is the first Nigerian to gain a Ph.D. in Physics. Another Professor – an Old Boy – will be honoured with A.D.C. (Distinguished Conqueror Award).

This will be the first time that your first Principal does not know personally the distinguished lecturer. You are welcome, Sir.

The topic is "Education, Yesterday Years, Today, and Tomorrow."

I do not want to pre-empt one iota what the lecturer will say in his lecture, but I will still say that the vast majority of those educated "Yesterday Years" were educated on a par with the present school system.

Long before I came to Nigeria in 1941, there was a Rev. Father Stephen Woodley, SMA, born in 1887 at Chester in the Diocese of Shrewsbury, England. He came at a time when nearly all the priests were continentals. The colonial Government launched great pressure on the missionaries to supply English-speaking priests and Reverend Sisters, capable of running good schools. Fr. Stephen Woodley was there-and-then appointed in charge of the Catholic schools in Lagos and environs. The imbalance in the number of Catholic schools and the Government schools soon became very apparent. There were 34 schools with nearly 4000 pupils only. Eleven of these schools were under the colonial Government.

The Head Masters and the teachers were certified native teachers, but in the Girls' schools, each student was taught by a European Sister.

In the Grammar School (at Holy Cross), Rev. Fr. Herber, SMA, taught Latin and French languages and the Principal, Fr. Woodley himself, took higher classes in the different English branches.

Herewith, a sentence recorded in the Archives: 'The Catholic Schools in Lagos can compare favourably with the best schools in the country and our boys are admired by all ... for their spirit of obedience and discipline.'

The above were the children of "Yesterday." What of the children of "Today"? They were more fortunate. Our children of "Today" received a more thorough education parallel with the English school system.

The archives tell us that Father Woodley held that post up to 1927 and enjoyed good health. He set a glorious example by building new schools and colleges, taking an interest also in games, especially in soccer. Unfortunately, in that year 1927, he was injured in the back and had to return to England.

At that time, both the policy of the Church and the colonials realized that education must be urgently pursued. Many young Catholic priests gave their lives, stricken down by Yellow Fever,

Black Water Fever, and Malaria, having lived only for a few years in tropical Nigeria.

Yet, it could be said that the pupils of "Today" (1930-1960), both at the primary school level, the secondary school and teacher training levels rivaled the colonial efforts to give a decent education to the rising generation at that time. Our products of "Today" became the basic rock of future education as we sailed into the education of "Tomorrow."

At this stage – the year of Independence 1960 – Nigerians took charge of their own country and initiated a new and most daring education policy. The third education "Tomorrow" had arrived.

There is no need to deny the fact that here in Nigeria, we followed step-by-step, the British Education Policy, punctuated with ultra-modern ideas borrowed from America and Europe. No longer did the new Ministry of Education confine our children to nine subjects. Even at the primary level, there were splits and choices up to twenty subjects. Every big subject was shrunk and all were added to the School Certificate Examination for the secondary schools; for boys and girls.

All of us now know that there are very obvious weaknesses in "Tomorrow's" education system, but let us leave that to our distinguished Physics lecturer. Please enlighten us all on Education "Yesterday Years, Today, and Tomorrow."

We anticipate you will write your own name in the pages of history by an honest analysis of nearly 140 years of education. Undoubtedly, you will lift the veil that has clouded our thinking in the past and brighten the future of the present student body.

We hope that their future will be brighter and also the future of the parents who are dedicated to give the best to their children.

We pray that those in administration will be honest and not afraid to purge the canker worms that have eaten into our present efforts. After all, education is the light of the world. May it shine on all of us."

Chapter Ten
Personal Testimonies

R. T. N. Onyeje
"What Rev. Fr. Slattery Taught Me"

I lost my parents at a tender age. As the Biblical saying goes, "Strike the Shepherd and the sheep will be scattered." At the demise of my parents, the children were scattered to different relations. And so, death robbed me of my parental guidance and counseling at an early age. The lot later fell on my eldest brother to take care of me; he became the beacon of my hope. Understandably, he was not well equipped by nature, being a man, to play the full role of parent. I must thank God, however, that his educational obligations towards me were religiously discharged. But the usual fraternal relationship between brothers was missing because he was a devout believer in the maxim: "Spare the rod and spoil the child."

An ideal environment for assimilating my true lessons of life was created when I got admitted into St. Finbarr's College when Rev. Fr. D.J. Slattery was the founding principal. In the course of conducting his lessons on religious knowledge, he used to digress a great deal into diverse subjects such as Moral Ethics, Pilgrimage to the Holy Land, Dignity of Labor, Football,

Hitler's submarines and his aerial bombardments during the W.W. II, et cetera. I enjoyed and benefited tremendously from these digressions because it afforded me the opportunity to entrench in my young mind those values that would serve to improve the quality of my future life.

From Father's speeches, sermons, reproaches, and commen-dations, he unwillingly taught me many edifying ways of life. He taught me that the youth would become the leaders of the society. He would not entertain any alibi from me. He once pulled me by the shirt to lower my face to his level and buffeted and battered my face; short of giving me a black eye. He then fired, "One more report, and you are thrown through the corridor of no return." I was happy, however, because if Oga had not executed the punishment himself and decided to march me to his sergeant "Kolofo", Mr. "E", I would have cursed the day I was admitted into St. Finbarr's College. It would be of interest to know that Mr. "E", loved and applied the cane in a very forceful manner, with an inexplicable delight. At the end of the "touch your toes" exercise, if you had any strength left in you to look up, you would notice a smile of ridicule on his countenance.

On Discipline and Honesty, Father taught me that one has to be very disciplined and forthright before one could be called a disciplinarian and a leader. That was why discipline was the pivotal "sine qua non" at the school. During our days, if you were caught indulging in any fraudulent practice at the examination hall, you would have attracted to yourself an outright and irreversible expulsion. The West African Examinations Council was aware of the integrity and scrupulous honesty of the man at the helm of affairs at St. Finbarr's College (one would expect no less from a Catholic priest) and it wasted no time in granting formal approval for the college as centre for its school certificate examination. Father did not condone any act of undisciplined behaviour from his students, or even staff. If you were caught shabbily dressed in school uniform, even after school period, you would not go scot-free. Father also taught me that rules and regulations made for all, are not bent; they must be seen to apply to all and sundry. Once you flagrantly broke any of the four commandments of the college, even if you were the Pele of the college football team or the grade one prospect of an impending external examination, boy, you were a goner. You would be marshaled through the dreaded "corridor." No mercy, no "Egunje."

In conclusion, I am deeply grateful to Father Slattery for his positive influence on my life and lives of all others who providentially received their spiritual and moral growth from him. My fellow retired conquerors who I spoke with, attested to the high level of discipline that Father had implanted in their young lives, which they have been striving to live up to. We all love you, Father. I thank you immensely, Rev. Fr. Dennis Joseph Slattery, for everything.

F. B. A. Ogundipe
"St. Paul's School Apapa Road Sports Field – A Handiwork of Rev. Fr. D. J. Slattery"

Besides founding Saint Finbarr's College in the year 1956, the name of very Rev. Fr. D.J. Slattery is linked with the founding of other institutions such as SS Peter & Paul Somolu, St. Gabriel, Bariga, St. Dennis, Akoka, St. Flavious, Oworonsoki, etc., to mention a few. However, the deep involvement of this clergy/ football administrator would not have been completed without mentioning a sports field constructed by him.

As already established, St. Finbarr's College was opened on Tuesday, 10th January, 1956, and it could be rightly said that playing of the game of football commenced simultaneously. The premises being used were St. Paul's Primary School, Apapa Road, our old or borrowed site. The field was very bushy and thorny and as such accommodated some dangerous reptiles and even scorpions in the water-logged zones.

The type of ball played by us at that time was either a tennis ball or Olympia popularly called "Bombom." These two balls would bounce well in the thick and uncleared field, nevertheless, the enthusiasm of the soccer-loving pioneers made the founding principal Very Rev. Fr. Slattery to think about the idea of transforming this thick bush into a befitting football/sports field. And uppermost was the thought that one day this might be useful in setting up a mini sports field which would stand the test of time for all to come. This field later became St. Paul's football ground Apapa Road, Ebute Metta.

Some time around 1996, I happened to pass by St. Paul's School Apapa Road, when I saw a mammoth crowd watching a football match. I, being a football enthusiast myself, was eager to join the spectators, not only to watch the match but to see what change or changes that might have taken place after some forty years that we left Apapa Road. Many structures have sprung up here and there in addition to the twenty room apartment that we used to know. I also noticed the five classrooms given to us by our host, St. Paul's School, through the then Manager Rev. Fr. Florence Macathy S.M.A., which served as classrooms, staff room, bookstore, clerk's office, and the principal's living rooms. The field looks exactly the same as it was in 1956. How did Fr. Slattery achieve this? He achieved this within a span of four months. First, he quickly organized a general manual labour on a daily basis for all the students. The first two weeks of our resumption was spent in clearing the proposed field and this period tallied with the Queen's visit to Nigeria in January 1956. St. Finbarr's College with number 162, was to take part in the Youth Week Parade slated for Saturday, February 11th, 1956. Within a fortnight, the surroundings of the field had been completed and we were privileged to use it in preparation for the match-past with a policeman in attendance.

The school went on short vacation during the Queen's visit to reopen again on Monday, 13th February 1956. Clearing of the field now became a regular exercise and as a punishment for erring pupils. The first two pupils to serve such punishment were Masters Chike Igbonoba and Albert Jemade. These two refused to sweep the classroom after closing hours as ordered by the class prefect, Sylvester Ogunamana. At that time, the class prefect reported the case to the principal, who surprised everybody by announcing the dismissal of these two students. But he later rescinded his decision by ordering the sentence of two weeks manual labour which would result in them clearing a quarter of the field. And moreover because the Easter examination was near, they were to spend the holiday in serving their punishment.

When the school resumed for the second term on Monday 7th of May, 1956, a quarter of the field had been cleared in addition to the surroundings. The manual labour was extended to two hours daily and the fear of being expelled for not obeying the principal's order was instilled in us. So, "afraid" was the watch word under the supervision of our class master, Mr. Ferdinand Ejieke. Before we knew what we were doing, within a short spate of time, the whole area was cleared, all the unwanted personnel removed, thick grass uprooted, bald portions were covered with Bahama grass and watered regularly. Thus, towards the end of May, the field was ready for marking, the rain helping us indeed. At last there was the sign-post of "Keep Off The Grass" meaning a sports field was in the making. The field looked beautiful and safe for use. The undulating portions were leveled.

Two factors contributed immensely to the development of the sports field indeed. These were some sporting equipment obtained from the then NFA. In 1955, the popular King George stadium, now Onikan Stadium, was to be expanded and fitted with modern amenities. The old wooden goalposts were to be replaced with aluminum types. All the old items removed from the stadium were given to charity. St. Finbarr's College was one of such beneficiaries. We gained the whole field equipment from the corner flags to the wooden goalpost and the nettings.

Also in that same year, 1955, at the Accra Sports Stadium, the Ghana Black Stars in the presence of Dr. Kwame Osaghefo Nkrumah spanked the Nigerian Red Devils by 7 goals to nothing. This was the worst defeat ever suffered by our National Football Team. This sounds incredible but it is true and this worst soccer defeat suffered by our National Team caused the then NFA officials to be disbanded, so also were the players. The jerseys used were considered to have been soiled by that tally and were not to be worn again.

Ghana proudly fielded stars like goalkeeper Layea, skipper Braindt Dogo Moro, Obilitey, Adjei, Adu Odamatey, Salisu, Baba Yara, Acqua, Aggrey Finn, Ofei Dodo, Ghamfi, and others. These were great names in the 50s and that defeat meted to Nigeria made St. Finbarr's College to inherit those jerseys. Eventually, the name Red Devil was changed to Green Eagles before it was finally changed to the present Super Eagles. Those red jerseys were used for practice.

With the provision of all the necessary equipment, white paints and lime were provided for the painting and marking of the field. The field looked as if it was being prepared for a big football match. This was the birth of the St. Paul's Ground. This is one of the dreams of Very Rev. Fr. D. J. Slattery, unknown to many people.

The field was officially opened on Friday 29th of June 1956, which was the first day of St. Paul's Primary School. A football match was arranged between the host, St. Paul's and the tenant St. Finbarr's College, which resulted in a 2 – 1 win for the host.

The construction of the field was a great delight to the Headmaster of the St. Paul's school, Mr. Shote and Fr. Macathy, the manager. The field served a dual purpose that is, as a football and an athletics field, and both pupils of St. Paul's Primary School and St. Finbarr's College benefited tremendously from it. However, it is on record that we did not play any other match on this ground until we left finally for Akoka in January 1959. This was simply because we were playing away matches to selected teams like St. Gregory's College, Obalende, St. Leo's Teachers, Training College Abeokuta, Eko Boys' High School, etc.

As for athletics, we had our first inter-house sports on the field on Tuesday September 25th 1956. This continued every year until we finally moved to our Promised Land at Akoka.

Segun Ajanlekoko
"The Rev. Father Slattery I Knew"

The Rev. Father Slattery I knew commenced in January 1965 when I gained admission into Form 1 at Saint Finbarr's College, Akoka. Then, the road that led to Saint Finbarr's College was most unimaginable, absolutely impassable terrain, and at the end of that long winding road you would find the pacesetter and beacon to the great upsurge in educational setting in Akoka, which SFC pioneered in those days before the like of Unilag, Our Lady of Apostles, and Anglican Boys Grammar School joined the educational match.

Rev. Father Slattery was a very strict disciplinarian and very agile. I believe his stature and height (under 5ft tall) must have helped him to be able to move around very quickly. He was like a colossus those days, yet he had an accommodating manner. There were certain things he could not stand. They were:-

1. Lateness
2. Untidiness
3. Mediocrity

4. Lies.

He was a quick-witted fellow and so expected people that he had trained to be well at the top of their chosen professions.

Talking about lateness, I remember often, the story of "the last trip" (i.e., every day the school van did a round trip from Akoka to Yaba to bring students to the school 3 times in the morning). The last trip, which was the 3rd one, comes in about 7:50 a.m. By the time the last trip came in and school morning assembly commenced, Father Slattery would be found lurking by the gate to the school waiting for latecomers. Usually, the students are very smart, so they too usually bidded their time before coming in. But often times this lurking practice was so elusive that you hardly knew where he was after morning assembly. I can remember that often times he pounced on students and chased them as far as the present-day end of University road. Some he caught, some escaped. If you were caught, the Lord help you !

His first punishment was a slap and then you were sent to VP and senior tutor who were experts at caning unruly students. But more often, he sent people back home when they were late. Such was the fear that was instilled in those of us who were opportuned to have tutelage under him that punctuality was one of the first lessons each one of us had to learn when we got into SFC.

Lateness did not end with students alone. I witnessed teachers being shouted at to go back home once they were late. Inf act, it was imperative for the teachers to be at the assembly with the students. That was the order and discipline of those days! That was a great teacher, Father Slattery.

As for tidiness, the morning Assembly was really an opportunity after prayers for the Principal and Senior tutors to inspect students class by class while standing on the college ground to look at how clean your white uniform was; whether the nails are properly cut, shoes checked to see if properly polished. And for those who were adults (yes, we had some adult students in those days), they must be clean-shaven, school uniform must not be torn and nails must not be in terrible state. If any of the students was found wanting in this regard he was sent home to come back only when he had secured the proper attire.

Cleanliness and tidiness were a tall order that must be adhered to by the young ones in those days, when you consider the bad roads they must pass through before getting to school; especially during rainy seasons when it is very muddy. But here we are, Father Slattery still held on to seeing us very clean. Today, I can say, however, that this has rubbed off on us. I look down on people who are improperly dressed, as my perception of them goes down. I don't believe that you can be untidy and be responsible. Cleanliness is next to Godliness – that was the rule we were taught.

The consequences of not meeting with the standard expected by Father Slattery are:-

> Cutting grass
> Kneeling down for 1 hour with hands stretched up very wide.

Of course, in the football sports, during our time, we won the coveted trophy called the Principal Cup 3 times out of our 5-year stay in the college. In 1968 and 1969 we won it back to back. The team was so good that four of them were called up (right from High School) to play for the National team - the Green Eagles; viz. Emilio John; Ajibade, Peter Egbiri and Richard Ibeh.

Academic Prowess

However, one area, which often times, people overlook about SFC, when they talk about our prowess in football, is academics.

But it is on record that in those days whoever did not pass the promotional exams got expelled. So, if you got to Form 5 in those days you could rest assured that your WASC result would be good; for you would have passed through the screening process set up by Father Slattery.

In my own time, 65/69 set, we had the best result in the whole of Lagos State, next was Kings College. Out of 85 of us that sat for the WAEC, we had 31 grade ones. So, proficiency in education was a must if you wanted to be a friend of Father Slattery in those days, never mind being a very keen footballer.

For the record, the Rev. Father D. J. Slattery imbued in us steadfastness, diligence, faithfulness and noble heartedness! That has helped a lot of Finbarrians to be where they are today. The like of Prof. Badiru, Prof. Eleshe, Prof. Sonubi, Vice Admiral Patrick Koshoni Nze mark Odu, Dr. Wole Adedeji and a whole lot of others.

Donatus Oguamanam
"My Memory of Saint Finbarr's College"

Coming to St. Finbarr's College is perhaps one of the best decisions my parents ever made on my behalf. I was in Primary 5 when my parents started contemplating about my secondary education. As at the time of the discourse, the list of possible schools, in order of preference, had St. Gregory, St. Finbarr's College, Igbobi College, CMS, Methodist Boys High School, and King's College. King's College was the last because my father felt that only the children of the "connected" and "influential" stood a chance.

Following their research, I would assume, the list narrowed to three with St. Finbarr's College, St. Gregory, and Igbobi College, in that order. Well, I passed the examination and came to St. Finbarr's with my father on the day for interview. I recollect seeing Father Slattery on that day, but I cannot remember any encounter with him. The interview comprised written and oral sessions. At a point during the course of the interview, the interviewer wondered whether I would like to enroll into the technical or grammar program. The question was strange and I implored the interviewer to excuse me a minute to consult with my father who immediately opted for grammar; so began my story at St. Finbarr's.

Finbarr's was competitive. Finbarr's was fun. My first year was a disaster as I missed out on the top three spots. My confidence was shaken, but that would change in the subsequent years, thanks to my parents, my physics and mathematics teachers, and Father Slattery. I was a regular at Father Slattery's moral instruction class. There was no examination and grades were not awarded. One was, however, obligated to attend the sessions for numerous reasons.

The moral instruction session was a talk on current affairs, philosophy, theology, and sociology. In retrospect, I feel it was aimed at imbibing ethical principles and strongly defining what it takes to be a Finbarrian. Thus, it is no surprise that the first session was on the history of the College. It was in the moral instruction class that I first came across the difference between a failure and a success. The former, if I may paraphrase the blessed Father, is the one who has not risen from the last fall, while the latter is one who has risen one more than the falls.

We were told to depend less on others and more on our abilities. This is in accord with one of the school's four pillars: that one should fail honourably as opposed to passing dishonourably, i.e., by cheating. Hence, it was not uncommon to find rooms where an examination was being conducted to be momentarily without invigilator(s).

Father Slattery was evidently very proud of his accomplishments at St. Finbarr's College then and was even prouder of his plans for the future of the school. He spoke very passionately about the progress of the college in light of its short existence vis-à-vis the other older schools. He was convinced that Finbarr's had to be the best and Finbarr's was the best. His passion explains the agony he felt when he gave his swan song moral instruction class.

Father Slattery was not a happy man when the Lagos State government, under the governorship of Alhaji Lateef Jakande, in its wisdom decided to assume ownership of St. Finbarr's College and the rest of the Mission Schools. It is my view that he must have underestimated the intent of the government and decided to persevere until it became very lucid that there was little anyone could do about the development. Father left Finbarr's brokenhearted, stressing that one never made the weak strong by making the strong weak. This view has now been vindicated by time.

Mr. Kpotie was the principal when Father Slattery finally stopped holding moral instruction sessions. I was known to Mr. Kpotie for all the right reasons. However, I was caught outside school during break on my way to West African Examination Council's (WAEC) at Fadeyi. I was walking down the college road, heading towards the University of Lagos gate, reflecting on university life, when I was jolted to reality by voices from a car that had stopped beside me. Turning in the direction of the voices, I froze in the recognition of Father Slattery and Mr. Kpotie. They, and another teacher, were riding in Mr. Kpotie's car.

Being conversant with the rules of the school, I knew my fate and was wondering how I could write my examinations as an independent student since I am going to be expelled and I might not find admission in a comparable school. I was ushered into the car and nobody spoke a word to me until we arrived at the college. At this point Mr. Kpotie wanted to know what I was doing outside in complete school's uniform (I was wearing my cardigan) while Father Slattery, the martinet, watched.

I was in Class four and I told them that my parents wanted me to take the General Certificate of Education (GCE) examination in preparation for Class five's WAEC examination. I showed them the form I was going to submit and informed them that my parents were aware that I was going to submit the form during the break period because I come to school at about 7:00 a.m. and get home very late because I go to private lessons immediately after school. To my surprise, Father Slattery went into a discourse with Mr. Kpotie who directed me afterwards to undergo some punishments.

The joy that overwhelmed me by this singular act of kindness on the part of Father Slattery is ineffable. While I cannot explain this act, it is plausible to conjecture that he believed the veracity of my narration and perhaps considered my academic record. Whatever it may be, I remain eternally grateful.

I cannot remember all the stories from Father Slattery's moral instruction sessions, but the fundamental principles are still etched in my memory. Father Slattery, via the founding and excellent management of St. Finbarr's College, touched and is still touching many. I left the college with the tools to take on the world: a strong-willed but compassionate heart, a disciplined and prayerful mind, and a sound education.

In closing, I must mention that Finbarr's was so self-sufficient in experimental apparatus, especially basic things like potentiometer and rheostat that could easily be fabricated by the technical students and their supervisors, that the school supplied other schools during WAEC examinations. That was made possible by the foresight of Father Slattery.

Dr. John Nwofia
"My Saint Finbarr's College Experience"

It was with excitement and trepidation that I showed up for my first day in the 1975 form 1 class. I had chosen to be in the Technical section. So, I showed up embarrassingly with my father who felt I should not limit myself and had me transferred to the Grammar section. Before we met with him, I had watched this sprightly, smiling man in the priestly robe with his cane ushering parents and, obviously new students, to different teachers who had assembled in front of the academic staff room. We later met with Father Slattery and he effected the change for me. He personally walked me to my new classroom, Form 1B. We saw a lot of Fr. Slattery in our first year. Our class was on the ground floor of the Library building, which itself was almost directly adjacent to the staff room. We found out, soon enough, that we could not be rowdy in class without Fr. Slattery being aware. The lesson of the first few unlucky students was enough. It was in that first year that I saw how a smiling priest could wield his stick sternly but still be regarded fondly by all, even the students whose rear ends were still smarting from the stick.

We were all disappointed when the Gov. Jakande government waded into Missionary schools and took over. Father Slattery was relieved of his post as principal but remained as the Moral Instruction teacher. In the classes one could hear his frustration as he could only watch his beloved school sliding into mediocrity under government control. He would tell the story of his sojourn in Nigeria, how he founded the school, his roles in the Nigerian Football Association. Some of his best stories centered around history of the closeness and adversity (from football) between St Finbarr's College (SFC) and St. Gregory's College. It was ironical that Mr. Anthony Omoera (deceased) had been drafted from St. Gregory's to be Fr. Slattery's replacement at SFC.

The former Vice Principal, Mr. Kpotie, soon took over from Mr. Omoera as principal. We initially saw a bit of Fr. Slattery's style of management but this quickly disappeared to his own personal style. My year was unique as the last group to be welcomed by the Rev. Fr. Denis J Slattery to SFC. We remain for ever grateful for that privilege. As we celebrate our Silver Jubilee (Class of 1975/1980) we will honor the man whom we loved and feared, our parents respected and adored. It is easy to guess that over ninety percent of the students at SFC came in because of Fr. Slattery's style of discipline which was responsible for the achievement of the school in the West African School Certificate (WASC) examinations and in the Principal's cup football competition. SFC was synonymous with Fr. Slattery. You could not mention one without the other

Fr. Slattery treated every student equally. He did not care whether you were the Army General's son or the son of the driver. I personally witnessed him ordering out of his office an Army Captain who wanted his son, who did not score high enough in the Common Entrance Examination, admitted to the school. He did not care about the threats from the army officer. That was the style and courage of Fr. Slattery.

Philip Bieni
"Oga Taught Us Hard Work"

Oga, as we called him, will always remain a hero to all Finbarians. He taught us about hard work, persistence, prioritizing, and quality management of all our endeavours. He also inspired us to treat others as we would like to be treated.Oga always respected other religious groups. During our school days, he madeduty for all Moslems to leave school at 12 noon on Fridays for their prayer meetings at the mosque. He always maintained that all humans are equal in the eyes of God. Imy series of conversations with him at his convent in Ireland before his death. He told me how proud he was of all the achievements of all his boys all over the world. He added that helooking forward to going back to Nigeria as his final resting place. be highly missed. May his soul rest in perfect peace.

Chapter Eleven
The Road to the End

This chapter gives an account of how SFCOBA tried unsuccessfully to bring Father Slattery back to Nigeria. He had wanted to return to Nigeria to die. All efforts to convince the Catholic Mission to send him back to Nigeria in his final days failed.

Segun Ajanlekoko, Yinka Bashorun, and I visited Father at his Maryland (Lagos mainland) residence on his brief return to Nigeria in 2000 (?). When he was sent back to Ireland by the Church, he very much wanted us to visit him in his retirement home in Cork, Ireland. That visit never materialized due to logistical constraints. But we continued to communicate with him by phone and mail. That gladdened his heart until his death.

"My Last Encounter with Late Rev. Father Slattery"
by Segun Ajanlekoko

This short narrative by me shows in retrospect what could have been a befitting grand finale of the exit of the man called Father Slattery from mother Earth here in Nigeria, but it was not to be.

While in office as President of SFCOBA, I made it a point of duty on a weekly basis to visit him at his St. Denis Catholic Church Home, to exchange words as well sought his guidance on matters that concerned the school, (our Alma Mater) SFCOBA, Nigeria as a nation, life in general, and, indeed, my own private enterprises.

It was on one such occasion that I posed the question where he would like to be buried if in accordance with his wish he died in Nigeria. He told me that he would like to be buried in St. Finbarr's school compound. I quickly responded by asking him where in particular. He replied by saying that it should be inside the retirement home that was being built for him by the SFCOBA inside the school compound.

I further asked him which particular spot. He then got up and asked me to drive him to the school compound. There and then he pointed to a spot near to his prayer room. I conveyed this message to the generality of the Old Boys. Thereafter, it became a project, which all Finbarrians both old and young directed all their energies to ensure its success.

Unfortunately, after his 80th birthday in February 29, 1996, he was asked to retire and was sent back to Cork in Ireland where he began his ministry. But hope was not lost as it was on record that Father Slattery actually wrote his wish in his Will. I, therefore, took it upon myself to regularly keep in touch with him on a weekly basis through telephone calls and whenever I traveled abroad, especially to Britain, I ensured that I had daily conversation with him from London.

On one occasion I decided to visit him in Ireland to be accompanied by a wife of one of our 1st six member, Mrs. Beatrice Ozugolo, who Fr. Slattery introduced to me as a life saver and whom Father Slattery told me had never for once

79

failed to pay him a visit every month in Cork in Ireland. Her late husband was the 1ˢᵗ President of the SFCOBA.

Unfortunately, the visit was not to be because Father Slattery fell ill and was hospitalized. Whenever I phoned him in Ireland, our discussion usually centered around St Finbarr's College, St Finbarr's Old Boys, plus of course my family and my business. He was interested to know how the Old Boys were doing and whether they were contributing to the sustainability of the Association.

I remembered a famous statement of his, during one of such conversations. He said, "whoever contributes to the growth of his old association will never go in want; he shall be blessed in multiples for he has been faithful to the cause."

And then the end came in June 2003. I was in Europe and I tried to phone Father Slattery as was customary with me only to be told at the Seminary that he was in the hospital in an Intensive Care Unit he could not speak to me. I got back to Lagos on July 11 2003 to receive a message from a Rev Father, an Ex-Finbarrian who informed me of the passing on of the great man Rev. Father Slattery, the paternal Father we never had!!

Two things I think are worth putting down for the sake of posterity, which emanated from my discussion with him while, so to speak, he was in exile in Ireland:

1. The first one has to do with his abhorrence for what he considered a confinement and solitude in the Old Monastery in Cork. He was of the view that he did not belong there as most of the people who were there had gone senile and could not engage in meaningful discussions with him. Father Slattery, up to the end, had a very sharp brain and was very vibrant at his old age. And so he felt that birds of

different feathers were flocking together in the monastery!!! He wanted to get out!!!

2. The second has to do with his patent and uncompromised desire to come back to Nigeria to "live" out the rest of his life in Nigeria. We developed various strategies toward the realization of this dream. One of the strategies was to ask the Old Boys to write a letter requesting that Father Slattery should be released to us and assuring them in Ireland that he would be well taken care of by the Old Boys.

But it was not to be!!! The letter was never written before the demise of our dear Father. It is a collective guilt of all the Old Boys. So, our dear Rev. Father has passed on, unsung, by those who benefited tremendously from his benevolence, his tutelage, his priesthood and his fatherly advice.

But I know that Rev. Fr. D.J. Slattery has fulfilled his mission and would, no doubt, be working in the higher realms (the vineyard of the Father), where only those who have passed are granted the opportunity to belong. We salute your great spirit!!! Live on, our dear Rev. Fr. Slattery. I do hope that you enjoyed the 1st year anniversary celebration that was packaged for you in 2004. We celebrated with by slaughtering a cow!!!.

Chapter Twelve
Social and Education Commentary

by Joe Igbokwe

I am told that there are no accidental great men. All great men made themselves in their own image. That which they become, they first desired. The world is divided into people who do things and people who talk about doing things. People who do things have the capacity to inspire and mobilize the masses of the people. The world has found out that it takes good leaders to have a good society, good government, good schools, etc. Leadership is more than just ability.

It is a combination of courage, determination, commitment, character and ability that makes people willing to follow a leader. Every great leader has left in other people behind him an enduring legacy to hold on to and a vision to carry on with.

I read from a school of thought that we are evaluated and classified by four things: what we do, by how we look, by what we say and how we say it. A well-known historian, philosopher, H.G. Wells says "the true test of man's greatness is judged by two fundamental questions:

What did he leave to grow?

Did he start men thinking along fresh lines with a vigour that persisted after him?"

People have written books asking for the Rights of Man, and others have countered the books asking man to seek to earn his rights. According to the latter, we must begin with the charter of duties of man and there is a firm promise that the rights will follow as spring follows the winter. The lesson is that power goes with responsibility and that if we reconcile power with service we are surely on our way to a higher standard of leadership.

A good man, and one of the finest Nigerians in diaspora, the main author of this book, a family friend, Head of Industrial Engineering Department, The University of Tennessee, USA, Prof. Adedeji Badiru, asked me to contribute a chapter to this book from my National Vision perspective. I accepted the offer and went to work. In a letter dated Friday, June 18, 2004, the Professor gave me the picture of the man called Rev. Father Dennis Slattery. Let me take the liberty of quoting Professor Badiru.

"As you may know, Father Slattery had extensive involvement in the early politics leading to Nigeria's independence, sports, newspaper publication and most notably, education. Apart from being a Roman Catholic Priest, he played many roles in Nigeria. He was an activist for Nigeria's independence. He was a soccer coach and referee. He was a newspaper publisher and editor. He was a teacher, principal and served the government of Nigeria in many advisory roles in education and social issues. He was most widely known for his educational work at St. Finbarr's College, my alma mater. I am one of the prime beneficiaries of his contributions to educational establishments in Nigeria. This, I see as a blessing. Hence the choice of the title: Blessings of a Father. This has both a spiritual connotation as well as a

literal interpretation. That I am where I am today is a credit
to these blessings brought by the opportunity to attend St.
Finbarr's College under Father Slattery's tutelage."

I was also privileged to read the first draft and the updated and
edited draft of this book before going to work. I read everything
I could find on Father Slattery - everything about him from
newspaper columns, magazines, his autobiography, MY LIFE
STORY. I asked people who knew him and had personal contact
with him to educate me more. In the cause of my findings
I came across a man who was in a hurry to give leadership
direction, motivation, inspiration and momentum. I read about
his mission and vision in founding St. Finbarr's College. His
national achievements and contributions to project Nigeria from
1944 to 2003 when he died and his famous four commandments
of St. Finbarr's College, showcased the Rev. Father as a great
man with an infinite capacity to achieve results.

I came across his views on Nigerian politics, his views on
bribery and corruption, his secrets of success and his shrewd
antics to get the attention of his students. In this write-up, I will
discuss some of the great attributes of this Irish-Nigerian and
this foremost educationist called the Enyioha I of Oru, Ahiazu
Mbaise and the Oosi Olokun Ijio of Ile-Ife, why he founded
St. Finbarr's College, his vision for Nigeria, etc. What was his
suggestion on how to restructure Nigeria? What did he say on
bribery and corruption, secrets of success and other matters of
national significance? What will Nigeria do now to make sure
the dreams of late Father Slattery do not fritter away?

Father Slattery, The Educationist

As one of the frontline nationalists who gave good account
of themselves during the struggle for independence, Father
Slattery, a man with an eye for the future, had a vision of what
the new Nigeria will be like. He knew that when a school is

opened the prison gates are closed. He knew that the post-colonial Nigeria would require high-level manpower that will replace the departing colonial masters. He knew that to get those sound minds would require a sound school. Like the sage called Epictetus, Father Slattery believed that "We must not believe the many, who say that only free people ought to be educated, but we should rather believe the philosophers who say that only the educated are free."

Listen to Rev. Fr. Slattery on why he founded St. Finbarr's College:

> "Soon as I recognised that the colonial government was anticipating vast economic and technical changes in the richest of all their colonies - Nigeria. In the immediate future, England saw the necessity of expanded manpower to meet the anticipated post-war development. It also saw the need to prepare a middle technical manpower to replace the overseas ex-servicemen who were holding very lucrative posts in the corporations, e.g., the railway, oil companies, industrial development, and so on that could be filled by Nigerian employees at a much lower scale. After all, Nigerian workers were never paid expatriate allowances, travel allowances, housing allowances or supplied with residences for their families. Without the government informing us, we knew what was needed in this hour of history. There was only one such school planned to meet the demands of the future and it was offered to the Catholic Voluntary Agency. After all, the other agencies felt that they were not qualified to undertake it."

That was how St. Finbarr's College was founded in 1956 and 49 years after, the great school has continued to register its marks in the sands of times. The school has today produced very eminent Nigerian citizens like Professor A. B. Badiru, Admiral Patrick Koshoni, Mr. Tom Borha, Segun Ajanlekoko,

Mr Mathias Uzowulu, Nze Mark Odu, Mr. Adesoji Alabi, Dona Oguamanam, R. T. N. Onyeje, Major-Gen. Cyril Iweze, Prof. Steve Elesha, Dr. Francis Ogoegbunam, Mr Chris Uwaje, Mr Jimi Lawal, Coach Steven Keshi, Henry Nwosu, Mr. Benedict Ikwenobe, Mr. Nduka Ugbade, Dr. Segun Ogundimu, Dr. Wole Adedeji, Engr. Festus Orekoya, Senator Adefuye, Mr. Ben Chambang, Mr. Deoye Fajimi, Mr. Adesoji Alabi, Anthony Odugbesan, Engr. Fred Ogundipe, Dr J. A. Ikem, Col. Michael Olusola Akanji, Dr. Omokoya, Dr. John Nwofia, Mr. Philip Bieni, Mr. Sam Cole, and hundreds of others. The mission and the vision of Father Slattery were to join St. Finbarr's with the few existing schools then to produce the high level manpower that will take over from the colonial masters when they eventually depart. He made a great success out of it.

Father Slattery and Politics

During the years of the locusts when the military dictator, the late General Sani Abacha, was terrorising the entire political landscape, Father Slattery, in 1996 made very useful suggestions that are still relevant today date. He wrote in his autobiography, *My Life Story*:

What is my recipe for healing the wounds of twenty-six years of military rule and mere ten years of civilian rule? Here is my humble reply:

Thirty years ago, before the fragmentation of this promising country began, I suggested that there should be no more than about eight regions, stop multiplication of states that are eating the national riches of the country, the oil wealth and preventing economic investment to bring employment to the masses.

Turn the present thirty states and Abuja into eight regions and reorganize the district councils into local governments.

We just cannot afford the luxury of thirty state governments, thirty state parliaments, hundreds of commissioners and thousands of highly paid legislators. We are exploiting the God-given wealth of this country to enrich the rich and starve the poor.

Elect a strong central government and on merit.

Make military coups treasonable and punishable by long-term jail sentences. Confiscate all ill-gotten wealth.

Father Slattery wrote this book in 1996 and the Army left in 1999, leaving behind a battered, damaged, looted, disunited and disjointed nation. As at the time of writing this, some 400 wise men and women are putting heads together at the on-going National Political Reform Conference to re-design, reconstruct, reposition and re-invent Nigeria to meet the challenges of the 21st century. Nigeria is over-governed with about 801 governments in place. Government officials, their families, cronies, associates, hangers-on, who are not more than 5% of the nation's population, control nearly 80 per cent of the nation's resources. Pareto Law allows 20 per cent of the population to control 80 per cent of the resources. So, while the greater majority is wallowing in abject poverty, a few sit on the nation's wealth. Now, if we agree that Nigeria is not a rich country which is true, we need to cut our coats according to the size of our cloth. We need to urgently reduce our expenditure in the business of governance.

If you are running a factory and you are not making a profit, you need to look at your entire process.

Are there some workers who are not contributing to the company's profit and you have no courage to sack them?

Do the workers need re-training?

Are you selling goods to enable you pay your workers and make reasonable profit for your efforts?

I am of the opinion that government should be run like a business. If the delegates can muster the courage to listen to Father Slattery and deal squarely with the fraudulent structures that have wasted the scarce resources of this country for years now, we shall be better for it. If the delegates can tackle all the issues disturbing the peace of this nation with manly confidence and brutal frankness, Father Slattery, who worked tirelessly to get this country to work, will continue to rest in peace.

His Many Worries on Corruption

Another very big problem that gave Father Slattery sleepless nights in Nigeria was the issue of bribery and corruption. Shortly before he died, the Rev. Father screamed to anybody who cared to listen, "Look at Nigeria today, several years after independence. Today, sad to say, Nigeria is riddled with corruption from the top to the bottom. No segment of Nigerian society is free from the cankerworm of bribery that has eaten into the bowels of our nation."

President Obasanjo saw the rot and devastation that the scourge had brought to the nation when he came to power in 1999 and promised that it was not going to be business as usual. The late Senate President, Chief Chuba Okadigbo had to be impeached for corruption. In 2003 some prominent Nigerians were summoned for helping themselves to the public till to the tune of almost 2 billion naira, being part of the money meant for the 27-year-old National Identity Card project. The accused include former ministers, a serving minister and other prominent citizens. They are Hussaini Akwanga, minister for Labour and Productivity and former Permanent Secretary in the Ministry of Internal Affairs, late Sunday Afolabi, former Minister for Internal Affairs, and Okwesilieze Nwodo, former secretary of the ruling Peoples Democratic Party (PDP). Others are Mohammed Shata, former minister of state for Internal Affairs Ministry, Tumi Mohammed, former Director, Department of Civic Registration (DCR), Niyi Adelakun, former representative of SAGEM SA, and Christopher Agidi.

Akwanga's successor, Mrs. R. O. Akerele was later arrested and she was reported to have admitted receiving $500,000 in bribery. A former Inspector General of Police, Mr. Tafa Balogun, had to be sacked for corruption and he is now facing a 70-count charge. Recently, a Minister of Education, Professor Fabian Osuji was sacked for corruption. The current President of the Senate, Senator Adolphus Wabara has just been removed as the Senate President, making it the third Senate President to be removed since 1999 for the same offence.

It is disheartening to note here that the National Assembly has become the greatest obstacle in the fight against corruption in Nigeria since 1999. Iit was the late Chief Bola Ige of the blessed memory that first gave me a hint on the type of people we have in the National Assembly. Bola Ige told me, "Joe, you need to know the kind of people we have in the National Assembly. You need to see their demands. You should fight to go to the National Assembly in 2003. This nation must be saved."

When I was told then that large sums of money had to paid out by the Ministries to get their budgets approved, I never believed it. When I was told that even the presidency would have to part with millions to get the national budget to sail through, I never believed too. When Mallam El-Rufai raised an alarm that Alhaji Mantu and Senator Jonathan Zwingina demanded N54m in order to endorse him as a minister, they denied it.

When Hon. Yerima accused the National Assembly members of taking recharge cards from GSM companies, he was promptly suspended for one month. Stories have been told of how the National Assembly pad the national budget with billions of naira in order to have enough money to take care of themselves before the budget is allowed to sail through.

Professor Soludo's mandate to banks to raise their capital base to N25b in 2004 has been sabotaged by the National Assembly. After collecting huge sums of money from the banks, they now divided the banks into three categories; N5b, N10b, and N25b. I know a member of the House of Representatives from one of the zones in the South that has purchased about six houses in Abuja and other places within two years of sojourn in the House.

Nigerians also remember that the former Senate President, Chief Adolphus Wabara, pleaded for the understanding of National Assembly members because, according to him, "they are trying to recoup the money they spent during the elections." Governors in the South cart away something close to N30b of federal allocations every month and yet a visit to the zone shows little development. A Minister of State in the Ministry of Finance, Mrs. Nenadi Usman once alerted the nation that our governors and local government chairmen are siphoning the people's money outside the country. According to her, once the monthly allocation is released, the value of foreign currencies goes up.

It is not enough for us to plead with our creditors for debt relief, we must show that we are a serious people. Our governors and local government chairmen cannot continue to stash away billions of dollars in foreign accounts while we are asking for debt relief. Officials of World Bank, International Finance Corporation and the Paris Club are aware of these foreign accounts, and will laugh their heads off any time such a request is made.

There are other cases which time and space will not permit me to mention here. But the truth remains that corruption has become the biggest problem facing the nation. The states and local governments are still wallowing in deep corruption. It has stunted our growth for years. Money meant for development has ended up in private accounts and Father Slattery saw it and raised an alarm. The late Professor Bade Onimade said, "It has been estimated that between 1973 and 1995, Nigeria earned about five times the total amount of money that went into the US Marshal Plan for the reconstruction of Western Europe after World War II, yet Nigeria is crying for reconstruction 23 years after all that money." I make bold to suggest that the fight against corruption must be a collective responsibility. I enjoin well meaning Nigerians to rise up in support of the president to deal with this hydra-headed monster in order to free the funds needed for development. This is a task that must be done.

Father Slattery's Secrets of Success

In this season where many able-bodied Nigerians are looking for short cuts to success, Rev. Father Slattery warned that wealth is created by going under the engines where hands are made dirty. According to Father Slattery, "There is no secret about success. I do believe that success lies in acknowledging one's limitations and applying one's talent very well to whatever one is doing. Success, in my view, is about 80 per cent sweat and 20 per cent talent. Sometimes, geniuses fail because they cannot work hard while people of lesser talent succeed because they are hard-working. Nobody will ever die of hard work. A lot of people die of laziness, doing nothing and growing fat.

This is a lesson for those who want to pass exams without reading, those who want wealth without work, those who want to live in the best houses in town, drive the best cars and wear expensive clothes without knowing how to make a kobo through dint of hard work, those who waste away their youths only to become beggars at old age, and those who waste the precious gift of time on frivolities like 419 and what have you. Those who had the privilege of traveling to places like the United States, Germany, Japan, South Korea and few other places in Europe have acknowledged the obvious and painful fact that Nigerians are not working hard enough to build their country. Everybody wants to be an importer of foreign goods and yet we want our economy to grow. We want our currency to stabilize. We want jobs for our children and yet we do things that will jeopardize our economy. We want to be like Japan, USA, France, etc but we do not want to pay the price. We do not want to do what they did to become what they are today. Building a nation is not a tea party. It requires commitment and serious-minded leaders and followers.

Slattery's Antics to Make Students Pay Attention

Father Slattery was also known for what Professor Badiru called "shrewd antics" to get the attention of his students. I enjoin readers to read in this book the account of Professor Badiru himself in a sub-title he called the Immaculate Conception Question. It is a must read for teachers in our primary and secondary schools. It is a kind of teaching technique that will empower the students to strive for excellence. My father employed similar antics on his children when we were young. Once you came home with your results, my father would go straight to your scores in English and Mathematics. If you failed in both subjects my father would tell you at once that you were not in school.

It made most of his children excel in English and Mathematics. My penchant for mathematics and eventual training in Mechanical Engineering had its roots from my father's antics. I know a man who went to Navy School, Abeokuta to pick his son for holidays only to discover to his chagrin that the boy performed so badly in the examination. Out of annoyance, coupled with the strong desire to make the boy know that he was not happy with his result, the man left his son in school for three days when other students had gone home for holidays. That singular attitude of the father changed the son's life forever, as the boy later became one of the best students in that school.

I have heard stories of parents who are always in the habit of telling you how long their daughters' hair is and how beautiful they look. They will also tell you how handsome their boys are. But the same parents will care less if their children do not know how to conjugate verbs. The same parents will not sit down to teach their children how to joggle variables to achieve results or solve simple mathematical problems. A basic knowledge of Mathematics helps to build logical thinking. Without a logical thinking ability, children can quickly go astray. Parents should pay less attention to vanity and more attention to preparing their children for the challenges of life that they will face later on. The power of a man or woman is based on how well he or she uses his or her intrinsic intelligence.

Conclusion

The Irish-Nigerian Father Slattery came to Nigeria in 1941 as a Catholic Priest, founded St. Finbarr's College in 1956 and trained hundreds of minds. He played politics, managed football, managed a newspaper and carried out other wonderful projects too numerous to mention here. Dale Carnegie once wrote that there is an old saying he had cut out and pasted on his mirror where he could not help but see it every day: "I shall pass this way but once; any good, therefore, that I can do or any kindness that I can show to any human being, let me do it now. Let me not defer nor neglect it for I shall not pass this way again."

I can say at once without fear of contradiction that Rev. Father Slattery read the old saying and insisted on putting it to practice in Nigeria. A thousand years will pass and Nigerians will ever continue to take notice of the fact that a Father Slattery once passed this way and left an indelible mark in the sands of time. His great work in Nigeria will stand the test of time. To die completely is to be forgotten. When a person is not forgotten, he has not died. Father Slattery lives on. His enduring legacies live on. His vision for Nigeria and the Black man lives on.

Information Sources

Slattery, Denis J., My Life Story, West African Book Publishers Limited, Ilupeju, Lagos, Nigeria, 1996.

Official Commissioning of PTA Projects: Programme of Events, St. Finbarr's College, Akoka, December 16, 2004.

The Finbarrian: Official Newsletter of Saint Finbarr's College Old Boys' Association, Vol. 8, Jan. 1999.

Chapter Thirteen
Reunion 2012

It was all fun, games, and reminiscing chatter at the Inaugural Annual Reunion of SFCOBA-North America in Atlanta, GA on September 1, 2012. A formal meeting was held to kick off the reunion. There was a specially-crafted celebratory cake for the occasion. After nine months of preparation, the reunion went on without a hitch. **Otunba Anthony Awofeso** and **Professor Adedeji Bodunde Badiru** headed the chronology of the Boys in attendance with their Class of 1972 lapel pins. Great thanks and appreciation go to Kenny Kuku and the Atlanta hosting committee, who worked tirelessly to ensure a smooth and successful event. Kenny ensured that we were all identifiable throughout the city of Atlanta that weekend with our Finbarr's logo'd shirts and caps. A few Finbarr's rascals showed up from all over North America to relive their glory days of Finbarr's "rascalism."

Notable among this group was the famous "Like-a-Bull" (aka Likabu), whose real-name identity can be found in Finbarr's historical records of boys who were thorns in the flesh of Finbarr's administrators. A quick search among the insiders of the old Finbarr's era revealed the real identity of Patrick

Efiom, who is now Col. Patrick Efiom serving in the US Army Reserve. His case proved that rascalism reformed is professionalism achieved. Likabu kept everything lively and entertaining throughout the reunion. He told hilarious stories that kept everyone in stitches of laughter. He also led the group in singing several of the old Finbarr's football fight songs. The songs came in handy during the novelty soccer match against the Atlanta Green Eagles. Several spouses were also in attendance to share in the celebrate the glory days of Finbarr's College. Later in the evening on Saturday, Sept. 1, the dance floor of the hotel got polished with shoe polish with repeated sliding of dancers' shoes. Many previously under-utilized leg muscles got stretched again by body gyrations in response to rhythmic calls of the loud speaker of the DJ. Knees long used for leisurely walking got tested on the dance floor. The knees held up well under the watchful eyes of the several physicians among the Boys in attendance. Dr. David Toks Gbadebo was particularly concerned about the quickening pace of the dancers' hearts. Fortunately, there was no cardiac emergency throughout the dance sessions. The photos that follow tell only a small part of the full story. The boys danced the night away, not missing any musical beats, as if they were trying to make up for the lost opportunity of the Finbarr's days of "bone-to-bone" dancing in the all-boys school.

The highlight of the three-day reunion was the novelty soccer match between the SFC Old Boys and the Atlanta Green Eagles, a well-regarded soccer club in Atlanta metro. On the SFC side were three of the best players that ever played for Saint Finbarr's in her glory days of soccer prowess in Nigeria. Their rusted skills got revived, if only in two-to-three-minute spurts. Dribbling and tackling skills that had been shelved for decades were brought back down to the playing level to be revalidated. It was like opening a can of worms. We had never seen so many Finbarrians pleading for substitutes (for themselves) from the sideline. Stephen Keshi, a former Finbarr's player, who went on to coach the Nigerian Green Eagles national team, telephoned during the match and wasn't pleased with how the Boys were doing. His words of encouragement and hints of brilliance were not enough to rescue the day. The Boys could muster only one goal against their opponents, who scored three goals in quick succession. Of course, the coach of the SFC side, Kenny Kuku, blamed the loss on a biased referee. He must have been recollecting a quote (attributed to the Duke of Edinburgh) found in Father Slattery's autobiography, which says, "Football is as good as its referee. A bad referee can spoil soccer." Professor Badiru also participated in the novelty soccer match, where he introduced a new principle of the

Physics of Soccer - - - "avoid the ball." In the end, the victors and vanquished got together to celebrate the friendly match. It is a wonderful football world, after all.

Group Photograph of attendees at the SFCOBA-North America Reunion
Atlanta, Georgia, USA, September 1, 2012

Deji Badiru, making a point at Reunion 2012

Appendix

Selected Quotes from Father Slattery's Book, *My Life Story*, West African Book Publishers, Limited, Ilupeju, Lagos, Nigeria, 1996.

"The Queen of England visited Nigeria during one of those years. When I bowed and shook hands with the Queen, I was quickly passed on to the Duke. The Queen took much more notice of the ladies in the line. Apparently, the Duke knew about my association with Football and refereeing. In the short conversation we had he made a very profound statement that I often used afterwards with an air of pride. The Duke of Edinburgh said to me, "Football is as good as its referee. A bad referee can spoil Soccer."

"But what has happened to our beloved country, one of the richest gems of Africa? What has become of all our dreams? How many have paid the supreme price sacrificing their lives at home and in foreign lands to build a new Nigeria? Literally thousands died in Egypt, North Africa, Burma, etc.

Look at Nigeria today, several years after independence. Today, sad to say, Nigeria is riddled with corruption from

Deji Badiru

the top to the bottom. No segment of Nigerian Society is free from the Cankerworm of bribery that has eaten into the bowels of our nation."

"As a result of a lecture I gave one time when I blamed the budding political leaders that they had fallen very quickly for the flesh pots offered by the Colonialists by taking huge salaries as ministers with or without portfolios, (I stated that there was no Freedom in Nigeria but our neo-political leaders were dancing to the tune of the British overlords), the next day, I was on the receiving end of a few scathing remarks in the press.

One paper wrote, "Father Slattery must have been drugged or drunk. He could not see wood or the trees!!

But another paper replied, "Father Slattery is destined to be the 'Cardinal Minzenty' of Hungary to be sacrificed on the altar of British imperialism." I was neither. I was Catholic Priest that stood for freedom – freedom to worship the true God and to enjoy the good things of life."

"I always regarded the visit to the Holy Land as a gift from my people in Nigeria. Had I not come to Nigeria in the first place, I probably would not have ever visited those sacred places that are particularly dear to the Catholic Priest. Thank you Nigeria for this wonderful gift on my 11th birthday, when I turned 44 years old. Don't forget that I am a Leap Year Child."

"The Four Commandments of St. Finbarr's In Slattery's Time

Actually, there were "Four Commandments", not ten, strictly implemented to help maintain discipline. Any

100

student violating these rules went down that "Corridor of no return." This had become a catch phrase in the school. These were the commandments:

Any student caught stealing will be expelled.
Any student caught copying at examination time will be expelled. Any student that fails is automatically expelled. He is not allowed to Repeat.
Any student leaving the compound during school hours without the Principal's permission will be expelled.
Any student caught smoking or with drugs will be expelled.

These were often discussed as the moral pillars of St. Finbarr's College, and the key to our policy. Proved beyond a shadow of doubt after thorough investigation, there was no mercy shown, even to a Form 1 Boy if caught breaking these decrees."

Deji Badiru